Going Back to New Orleans

Post-Katrina Re-connections and Recollections

100% of author's royalties go directly to the United Way of Southeast Louisiana

Published in the United States by Nurturing Faith Inc., Macon GA, www.nurturingfaith.net.

Library of Congress Cataloging-in-Publication Data is available.

978-1-938514-36-4

DEDICATION

for my parents,
Bob and Barbara Montgomery

Two young recent graduates, raised in rural/small town regions of Mississippi, each one all alone, ventured by God's Providence into the big city of New Orleans—each had accepted academic scholarships to attend Tulane University. The two individuals met at a student fellowship one Sunday night at St. Charles Avenue Baptist Church, and, the rest, as they say . . .

ABOUT THE COVER PHOTO

The image of the piano and roses is courtesy of AJ Caruso. This is how AJ and his father found their father's piano—on it's side with the roses on the keyboard—when they returned to his father's house after Hurricane Katrina.

ENDORSEMENTS

Bert Montgomery's *Going Back to New Orleans* is more than just a collection of stories from those who lived through it and those who know the city well. As the subtitle suggests, it also tells the story of re-connections. Although I personally escaped the worst of Katrina's devastation, the devastation to my psyche was very real and I will never forget that smell of despair, both real and literal, after returning to the city. Bert's and his family's connections to the church I have attended for decades and most recently served as Associate Pastor, is a strong one... Not only did our connections with current and former members remain strong in the aftermath of Katrina, those connections were strengthened and many new connections were made through more than twenty work groups of youth, college students and adults who were housed and fed by our small congregation as they spread the love that Americans and Christians felt for their fellow citizens. As you read *Going Back to New Orleans* you will feel that you, too, whether you have ever been to New Orleans or not, share the story of a great American city and people who have re-connected to all that is truly important when tragedy strikes.

—Paul R. Powell, PhD, Associate Pastor,
St. Charles Avenue Baptist Church, New Orleans

As a lifelong resident of St. Charles Parish where Bert fondly recalls his youth, I lived and worked the aftermath and recovery that Southeast Louisiana endured. Each of these different accounts which surround the handling and horrors of one of the nations worst national disasters, is real and revealing. I felt myself relating to each as if I was living their ordeal through Bert's words. As a child, I knew and respected the Montgomerys. We were all a part of the First Baptist Church of Norco family. Bert was a few years ahead of me, both at church and at Destrehan High School, but I knew and respected him then as I do now. I am still a member of First Baptist and we still appreciate the contribution and influences that the entire Montgomery family made to our church and community. This book and its reflections are a contribution of what we have come to expect from Bert. If you want a true account of the struggles of everyday people after Katrina, read this book!

—Gary L. Smith, Jr., Louisiana State Senator

TABLE OF CONTENTS

Part Two: Hurricane Katrina Experiences, Continued
(Others' Stories)

Part Three: Full Circle in the Big Easy
(Final Words)

FOREWORD

by Mrs. Sandra Chaisson

Editor's Note: Bert's high school honors English teacher, Mrs. Chaisson, always insisted on calling Bert by his full first name: Robert. In high school, it used to drive Bert crazy. Today, he wouldn't have it any other way. Here is a foreword from ROBERT's teacher . . .

Hurricane Katrina made landfall in Louisiana on August 29, 2005. For New Orleanians and the people living in the surrounding parishes and southern Mississippi, the mention of her name, like traumatic events so often do, evokes feelings of sadness, sorrow, loss, and helplessness. Just a few minutes of small talk with total strangers will often wind its way to "where were you for Katrina" or "how did you make out in the storm?"

The Storm. Just say those two words in Louisiana and everyone will know you mean Katrina. In New Orleans, time itself is reckoned by The Storm. It has become our collective chronometer.

Robert Montgomery's *Going Back to New Orleans (Post-Katrina Re-connections and Recollections)* does a fantastic job capturing the angst surrounding the storm and the indefatigable spirit of the people of New Orleans. Always the music enthusiast, Robert chose to name his book after a song by the iconic New Orleans musician Dr. John. With music as his backdrop, Robert gathered stories from friends, both longtime and long lost, and orchestrated his opus of The Storm. The individuals who share their stories are unique, but the outlines are the same: hearing about the storm; deciding to leave for the storm; running from the storm; watching in horror as the area floods; returning to their own problems; the city pulling together with little help from the federal government; the New Orleans Saints; the Super Bowl.

Going Back to New Orleans is different from other books about Katrina. This book captures the singularity of our city and the passion it awakens in its people. Very few cities in the United States, and absolutely none of suburbia, can boast the uniqueness of the City that Care Forgot. The stories are all from Katrina survivors, all special, all real, and all compelling. It's a must read for other Katrina survivors because of the authenticity of each story. The experiences of others will certainly strike a similar chord with everyone who lived through The Storm. It's a must read for others who have yet to grasp the devastation The Storm leveled against Louisiana. While people in this area are truly grateful for the outpouring of monetary charity as well as "boots on the ground" charity from individuals and the church groups who came down to help us rebuild, there is still the feeling of abandonment. There are still clueless individuals who do not understand the sense of hopelessness of Louisiana and Mississippi residents. It's as if we were swept off to sea from the rest of the United States, both literally and figuratively.

Robert contacted me a few years back to thank me for being his English teacher for tenth and twelfth grades. He had just written a book of inspirational essays called *Elvis, Willie, Jesus & Me: The Musings and Mutterings of a Church Misfit*, a wonderful little book he put together using his love of music and an informed and enlightened Christian conscience. Robert asked me if I remembered him. I told him that, of course, I did. When teachers get together we always tell war stories of our time in the trenches. Robert's name always came up when I told one of my favorite, light-hearted stories:

> *In one of my English II Honors classes, I had three celebrities: Robert Montgomery, Cesar Romero, and Houdini. All in one class. It was hard at first to keep a straight face when calling the roll. Not making this up . . . true story.*

That bit of classroom history always elicits a chuckle or two.

A couple of years ago Robert and his two sons came by for a quick visit with me in New Orleans. He was floored when I told him that I always remembered him as a good student. He thought he was a terrible student. I remember a smart, inquisitive young man; he remembers a parent-teacher conference where his mother was told "Robert could be doing so much better." From a teacher's perspective, good grades are nice, but an intelligent, thoughtful student is preferable. I am writing a foreword for another of Robert's books. Obviously, only one of us was correct in our assessment of Robert as a student.

Mrs. Sandra Chaisson
English and Literature Teacher, Retired
Destrehan High School

FOREWORD

Dr. John D. Hendrix

I think I understand Bert Montgomery better after being reminded of Jeremiah 1:5, "Before you were formed in your mother's womb I knew you." Maybe I understand Jeremiah a little also. When my wife, Lela, and I arrived at New Orleans Baptist Theological Seminary and St. Charles Avenue Baptist Church in the early 1960s, Bob and Barbara Montgomery were a part of most programs going on at the church. I've often said that ninety percent of church life is just showing up, and Bob and Barbara always seemed to be around somewhere. This began our long history with most things New Orleans. It took Bert's invitation to write this foreword that started the connecting of the dots.

We had moved to Nashville, Tennessee, when Bert born in 1968—and we lost contact with Bob and Barbara. But, Bert emerged into my life when I left Southern Baptist Theological Seminary in 1996 to become pastor of Northside Baptist Church in Clinton, Mississippi. There was Bert, a member of the pastor search committee. Bert and I would have lunch periodically, and I suspected that Bert ate pizza (and only pizza) three times a day.

Lela and I were in Clinton when Katrina made its destructive march across the gulf coast in 2005. For six weeks we had people in our home from the devastation along the Louisiana and Mississippi coast line. These were people we had known since the 1960s, and they knew they were free to come seeking refuge, in spite of the lack of electricity in our home from Katrina damage.

While Lela and I were co-pastoring University Baptist Church in Starkville, Mississippi, during the first decade of the new century, Bert was a student at the Baptist Seminary of Kentucky, then located in Lexington. While there he came under the influence of David Adams—one of the brightest and craziest of doctrinal students I ever supervised at Southern Seminary. Along with David Cassady, another former student and the founder of the FaithLab, Bert began a career of writing and publishing (which I hope he will continue). Later, Bert followed us as pastor of University Baptist, Starkville.

Bert's current writing, using the ancient art of storytelling, reflects how intimately we are all connected. I imagine Bert has made this remarkable connection with the people of his past through Facebook and other "in touch" social technologies. Although these have opened up new ways of renewing relationships, I still prefer the sound of the human voice and the sight of the changing features of the human face. They come to me through daily walks and the night journeys of dreams and fantasies. I wake up, smiling, and think, "Wow, that was so and so . . . I wonder how they are doing." Sometimes I make a call. Once in a while I will see them. And then, I tell a story.

There is always some question about the accuracy of our memories. When we tell stories coming from those moving pictures on the screen in back of our eyes, our imagination is already at work. That's why my kids and grandkids say, "Papa, those stories just get better and better." The stories change as I go through different stages and transitions.

Memories are not exact copies of experiences deposited in a memory bank. They change significantly when they are pulled out of storage. That doesn't make us a pack of liars, though. We don't see past events as *they* were; we see them as *we* are—now. When caterpillars become butterflies, they would probably say that earlier they were just little butterflies—what happens is maturation. We can still maintain that the men and women of this book who tell their Hurricane Katrina stories get the chronicle of events mostly correct and intact, although a few specifics may be out of order, or there may be some embellishment. This is okay! Like all good stories, they will awaken your own memories.

I must also say something else about the importance of what Bert has done. We might call this "social capital," the value of accumulated relationships over a lifetime that get focused on the tragic outcomes of Hurricane Katrina. These stories didn't spontaneously happen. They had to be dug out of the memory banks of adolescence and young adulthood, and people had to respond in reciprocal relationships. Here is a rediscovery of a dense network of mutual bonding and trustworthy obligation. Bert issues an invitation and people respond.

For most of my 78 years, the strong bonds of community rode a tidal wave of deeper engagement. But for the last twenty years, something has happened. Silently, and without warning, that tide changed and was reversed, overtaken by a rising current of isolation and individualism. I'm not making this up—there is plenty of evidence, individually and corporately, of being *alone*, together. This book of personal stories seeks a different current.

Dr. John D. Hendrix
Baptist Pastor, Retired; Professor of Christian Education, Retired;
Youth Minister at St. Charles Ave. Baptist Church, New Orleans, 1963-1966

INTRODUCTION

Hurricane Katrina passed over the New Orleans area on Monday, August 29, 2005 (the Mississippi Gulf Coast took the most direct hit). That day, and in the days, weeks, and months that followed, I became acutely aware of a deep, wide chasm in my life that previously I had rarely, if ever, noticed.

On March 14, 1968, at Baptist Hospital in downtown New Orleans, I was born. I soon joined my older sister, Becky, and our parents, at a house on Jade Avenue, just off West Metairie Boulevard, in Metairie. I have almost no recollection of living there. When I was three years old, we crossed over West Metairie and over David Drive and moved into a house on Abadie Avenue (walking distance from LaFreniere Park). Then, in 1978, my parents moved our family out of Jefferson Parish. We headed west on Highway 61 (Airline Highway) into what seemed at the time to be in the middle of a swampy nowhere. We turned left in St. Charles Parish at the newly-developing Ormond Estates, drove literally right down to the Mississippi River, and turned left again on River Road. On our left were neighborhoods and houses. Directly to our right was the levee—and on the other side of the levee was the Mighty Mississippi. (By the way, at certain parts of the drive along River Road in St. Charles Parish, you can look up—yes, *UP*—from your car and see huge ships from all over the world). We turned left yet again by a small brick building, which was then the United States Post Office in Destrehan. It was in that Destrehan neighborhood, on Ormond Oaks Drive, that we settled in for the next seven-and-a-half years.

We began attending church at the First Baptist Church of Norco (just follow River Road as it curves in a north-westerly direction). Becky and I attended John Curtis Christian School in River Ridge back in Jefferson Parish (just follow the river eastward). Becky graduated from Curtis in 1982, the same time I graduated from eighth grade. She left for college, attending Mississippi College up in Clinton, Mississippi, and for my four years of high school, it was primarily just Mom, Dad, and me. After ninth grade, I transferred from Curtis to Destrehan High School which was walking distance from our house on Ormond Oaks Drive (if you cut through neighbors' yards, jumped a ditch, cut through strangers' yards, and crossed a few streets).

All the while, Dad worked for Wand Rubber Stamp Works, Inc., on Magazine Street in New Orleans, a few blocks from Canal Street. By 1975 he was president and co-owner of the business. By the time I started tenth grade at DHS, Wand had moved into a new building in Kenner—it was sandwiched between Williams Boulevard and the New Orleans International Airport.

In 1986, Dad—after over thirty years in the New Orleans area—decided that with Becky graduating from college and with my graduating from high school, it was time for Mom and him to move again. Dad sold his share of the business. I graduated from DHS, and two weeks later we moved to Tennessee. Ever since then, I've lived outside of Louisiana.

This book is a collection of stories about New Orleans and the surrounding region. These are my parents' stories—both of them are from rural/small town parts of Mississippi, and they only ended up in New Orleans by chance (or, as I prefer, by the hand of God). These are my stories as an adult coming to terms with and trying to bridge the chasm that separated my first eighteen years of life from my entire adult life.

But most importantly, these are the stories from my Louisiana friends, classmates, members of my church family, etc., as *they* come to terms with and bridge the chasm that divides their lives into categories called "Pre-Katrina" and "Post-Katrina."

These are stories of living in, being removed from, and ultimately going back to . . . *New Orleans.*

PART ONE

Crescent City Callings

(My Stories)

Remembering . . .

The entire week after Katrina hit and the levees broke—I was in a state of shock, though I didn't really know it at the time. I hadn't lived in the region since the very end of May, 1986; nineteen years had passed by August 2005, and I had now lived outside of Louisiana longer than I had lived in it.

In northern Kentucky, that week went on as usual for everyone . . . except for me. Saturday night came around, and I had still not been able to prepare a sermon for Sunday morning. I awoke about 4:30 a.m. Sunday, and these thoughts just poured through my fingers onto the page. That morning's "sermon" was this very personal reflection on the week's events.

I later edited it into the form of a musing, and it appeared in my first book, Elvis, Willie, Jesus & Me. *Because of its relevance to this collection, Smyth & Helwys Publishing graciously granted permission to include it here.*

Again, this was written in the early morning hours of September 4, 2005—the weekend after Hurricane Katrina hit the Gulf Coast.

Remembering. Sometimes we call it just being nostalgic, a melancholy moment of escaping back into the past. But it's not simply that; at least not most of the time. Remembering somehow calls up from deep within us that which we are, that which has shaped us, influenced us, and that which is still shaping and influencing us even now, though we may not even be aware of it. I have been doing a lot of remembering this week. A *lot* of remembering.

Remembering short family trips to the Mississippi Gulf Coast—Biloxi and Gulfport and Mobile, Alabama—where we did "touresty" things and swam in the Gulf of Mexico.

Remembering going with my dad to Wand Rubber Stamp Works, Inc., the business in New Orleans, on Magazine Street, of which he was President and Co-Owner. He would take me with him some Saturday mornings, and I'd earn a little money sweeping stairs and cleaning windows. Then I'd go look for rats on the largely vacant third and fourth floors of this historic very old uptown building. Remembering that Mr. Sal and Little Sal, Kenny, Clinton, and Mrs. Marie were not just people that worked with Dad, but that they *are* lifelong family friends.

Remembering the schools I attended: Airline Park Elementary in Metairie; John Curtis Christian School in River Ridge; and Destrehan High School, in, of course, Destrehan.

Remembering my church: First Baptist Church of Norco (NORCO—New Orleans Refinery Company) and Bro. Jimmy Knox who baptized me there. Bud Granier and Pam Smith and Kirk Banquer—my Sunday School teachers.

Remembering high school—too many memories, if that's possible. Great teachers like Ms. Bourgeois and Mrs. Chaisson and Mr. Charles Catalano, the band director. Teachers that took a great interest in their students, or at least in challenging *this* student.

Remembering my neighbors, my church family, and friends at school: the Graniers, the Vitranos, the Robicheauxs, the Schexnaydres, the Cambres, the Caughmans, and Mary, Marta, Debbie, and Ronny. I have maintained some level of regular, sometimes frequent, contact with only a few them since I moved away in 1986—and in the past few years even that has been far too sporadic.

Remembering playing trombone in the historic St. Louis Cathedral in the French Quarter, and marching numerous times inside the Louisiana Superdome—even at the halftime of a New Orleans Saints game.

And remembering only evacuating New Orleans *one time* for a hurricane. All other times, we stayed put. I remember specifically a smaller hurricane when I was probably about seven or eight years old; I helped Dad put masking tape on all the windows to keep the glass from shattering, and then we all sat close together inside the house. I clearly remember walking outside into my front yard during the eye of the hurricane—a dead calm . . . a most eerie feeling.

I remembered all of this and so much, *so very much* more this week as I have obsessively followed the news, checked internet websites, and made hundreds and hundreds of attempts to contact friends and neighbors—

all in vain. Today, I have no idea how they are, or where they are, or whether or not their houses were damaged or destroyed.

But this is not simply nostalgia. No.

Remembering all of this is summoning up inside of me the core of my being. This is *who I am.*

The New Orleans area and its people are an essential part of my very being—having shaped and influenced me directly for the first eighteen years of my life, and still shaping and influencing me today, though I may not always be aware of it.

Remembering . . .

Thank God . . . and/or Greyhound

(By Bob Montgomery)

Dad was born out in the countryside of Lincoln County, Mississippi. He graduated from Brookhaven High School at age sixteen, and was offered a full scholarship to attend Tulane University.

I asked him to share his story of how he ended up in New Orleans . . .

In July of 1953, during the summer of my sixteenth year, I took a one-day trip from Brookhaven to New Orleans, a distance of 130 miles. That was more than twice as far as I had ever been from my birthplace in Lincoln County, Mississippi. During my high school years I had been on a few school activity trips to places as "distant" as *sixty* miles from Brookhaven!

I had graduated from Brookhaven High School that spring with a scholarship offer to attend Tulane University in the fall. With no knowledge of either Tulane or New Orleans, a high school friend (Dan Day) and I made plans to go by Greyhound bus to New Orleans and look around. On a weekday morning in July we left Brookhaven about 7:30 a.m. on the Greyhound Express. The bus made one scheduled fifteen-minute rest stop at the Hammond bus station, then it proceeded south on U. S. Highway 51 through Manchac Swamp to LaPlace, where Highway 51 merged with Highway 61 and continued on to our destination. The trip took almost four hours in those days.

We caught our very first glimpse of the downtown New Orleans skyline as the bus reached the top of the overpass at Carrollton Avenue and descended onto Tulane Avenue for the final twenty or thirty blocks to the Canal Street bus terminal. We were already well aware that we were not in

Brookhaven anymore by the size of the city and the tall buildings in the business district. As we started toward the door of the bus terminal leading out to Canal Street, a cab driver opened the door and, holding it open for us, he casually asked, "You boys lookin' for a woman?" Those were the very first words we ever heard addressed to us in New Orleans! We simply turned away from him and quickly started walking toward the busy shopping district along Canal Street.

At the second intersection from the bus station, we spied a jungle scene painted on the whole side of the corner building. It depicted trees and vines with monkeys swinging among the branches. The sign out front identified this establishment as "The Monkey Bar." It was late in the morning, and the front doors were open. A couple of men were cleaning and mopping the floors, and, as we passed by, we caught a whiff of the stale alcohol-tobacco interior of that barroom.

Dan and I never made it to the Tulane campus that day. We didn't even get off Canal Street! The distance from the bus station to the foot of Canal Street at the Mississippi River was about fifteen blocks. We marveled at the numerous department stores and other businesses up and down the wide street with the "neutral-ground" in the middle. The Canal streetcar line ran down the neutral-ground. At the "foot" of Canal Street we glimpsed the Mississippi River at the Eads Plaza overlook.

We had noticed some large movie theatres a couple of blocks from the bus station. In the early afternoon we attended a matinee showing at the massive Saenger Theatre inside of which several of our Brookhaven picture shows could have been placed. The newly-released movie, *Houdini*, starring Tony Curtis and Janet Leigh, was playing. After the movie, we went back across the street to the bus station and boarded the return Greyhound Express northward to Brookhaven. We arrived back home shortly after dark.

Three or four weeks later we made the trip again, with the express purpose of finding our way to Tulane. Once we arrived back on Canal Street, we determined that the St. Charles Avenue streetcar ran right by Tulane. We boarded it, paid the seven-cents (each) fare and started out St. Charles Avenue. It seemed to us to be such a long way from Canal Street to the Tulane campus (it is about three miles). We got off the streetcar at the main entrance of Tulane, which is across from Audubon Park, and walked through the quadrangle to Freret Street and turned back to St. Charles. The campus was deserted during the summer break. We caught a streetcar back to Canal Street, saw another movie, then boarded the Greyhound back to Brookhaven again.

On those two one-day trips, Dan and I had experienced a mere inkling of the vast difference between Brookhaven and the city of New Orleans.

Daddy drove me back to New Orleans on September 14, 1953, and I enrolled as a freshman student at Tulane. It was only after 32½ wonderful and eventful years that I left the New Orleans area again (this time along with Barbara, Becky, and Bert!).

It Happened on St. Charles Avenue, Part I

(By Barbara Montgomery)

My mother was born and raised on a Mississippi Delta farm south of Dundee, Mississippi. She graduated from Tunica County High School and journeyed not too far southward to Clinton, Mississippi (just west of Jackson). There, she attended Mississippi College for four years—a college owned and operated by the Mississippi Baptist Convention. Majoring in Latin, she planned on teaching the language after her graduation.

Instead, she found herself in a strange and faraway land . . . Here is Mom's account of how she ended up in New Orleans, and how she met my father.

Early in my senior year at Mississippi College, I realized that for the first time in my 21 years of life, I did not know what I would be doing the next year. Not feeling ready to face a classroom of high school Latin and English students each day, I decided to go to Ole Miss Graduate School. When my Latin professor, Mr. Thomas Boswell, and my Faculty Advisor, Dr. Charles Martin, learned that I intended to go to graduate school, they both *insisted* that I apply to Tulane (both of them had graduate degrees from there).

To satisfy them, I applied to Tulane in addition to Ole Miss; all the time planning to go to Ole Miss. Sometime later, I received a letter from Ole Miss stating that graduate-level Latin courses would not be offered the next year. That same day, a letter came from Tulane offering me a full scholarship.

I could not imagine going to a place like New Orleans all by myself! However, Daddy and Mama felt that we at least had to check it out. So, in

April 1961, they took me to New Orleans for the first time. We met with the Classical Language professors at Tulane, and, almost before I realized what was happening, it was settled that I would enroll in Tulane that fall.

Since Tulane was still primarily an all-male university with no dormitories for women, we had to find an off-campus place for me to live. In July we went back to New Orleans and located the Park View Guest rooming house on St. Charles Avenue—just two blocks from the campus. But, I still did *not* want to go to New Orleans. It seemed I was being carried there by forces beyond my control. All summer I cried, and I cried—until I was sick. For weeks I had to have B-12 shots to build me up.

On Tuesday, September 12, Daddy, Mama, and I went again to New Orleans, this time supposedly to leave me. I moved into the Park View Guest House, and on Wednesday morning, I registered at Tulane. When Daddy and Mama got ready to leave, I cried so much Daddy agreed to let me go back home, since I did not have classes until Monday, September 18. Before leaving New Orleans, he made my return plane reservations from Memphis to New Orleans for Sunday.

I was okay again—until Sunday afternoon, September 17, that is. Uncle Elmer and Aunt Eula Pegram rode with us to the Memphis airport, and I cried so hard that Daddy had to *push* me onto the plane. I was scared to death—what was I going to do when I got off that plane? How was I going to get to the rooming house on St. Charles Avenue? (I did not know how to hail a cab.) Somehow, I did get one and arrived there safely. This was late on the Sunday afternoon. A few minutes later, I walked one block to the St. Charles Avenue Baptist Church for the evening Training Union meeting. Someone took me to the college department, where a deacon was speaking on the role of a deacon in the church.

When the invitation was given at the end of the evening worship service, I moved my membership from the First Baptist Church in Clinton. A tall, good-looking young man in the greeting line asked if I knew Norman and Marleen Gough who had just moved up to Clinton and Mississippi College. I did not. Later, I learned that person's name was Bob Montgomery.

Had the term "culture shock" been around in 1961, it would not have begun to describe how I felt those first few weeks in New Orleans. My entire life had been spent in the safe confines of family, church, and a Baptist college campus. Not only were the Louisiana people different from me, they spoke with a *very strange* accent. Here, *I* was the *different* one!

The rooming house was home to working single people, high school and college students, graduate students, and a few retired people—but no other Baptist girls! I shared a room with a "thirty-something" Cajun woman from Houma. Our suitemates were two teenage girls, whose father worked in Venezuela with an oil company. They attended Catholic girls' schools. Despite our cultural and age differences, we four became good friends.

Not only was I in a different culture, I was on my own for the first time in my life. Daddy was about four-hundred miles away. But, God had placed someone special there for me—the next week Bob Montgomery called and asked me to go with him to the Tulane-Florida football game on October 6. Other football games, concerts, church socials, etc., followed. And, by the Thanksgiving holidays, I did not want to leave the city that I had tried so hard to stay away from.

It Happened on St. Charles Avenue, Part II

(by Bob Montgomery)

Dad had already been in New Orleans for a few years—even his parents and his younger brother and sister had moved down into an apartment off Lee Circle for a short while. What follows is his account of how he met my mother . . .

Though I had been in New Orleans since 1953, it was in the summer of 1958 that I moved my church membership to St. Charles Avenue Baptist Church. During those early years I was a member of Coliseum Place church on Camp Street, just a few blocks uptown from Lee Circle. A very good friend in the Youth Department there was Bobby Armstrong (whose son, Danny, later attended John Curtis with Bert).

By my junior year at Tulane, I had become more and more active in the Baptist Student Union on campus, and most of the students there were members of either St. Charles Ave. or First Baptist. Gradually, I began to attend more functions at the BSU and the student-emphasized ministries at St. Charles. Friends there included Norman Gough and Dan Barkdull (who had originally invited me to come to weekday lunches at the BSU Center just off campus on Freret Street).

After graduating from Tulane in 1957, I worked for a year at Wand Rubber Stamp Works, then joined the Air Force Reserve and spent six months on active duty in 1958 (about two months at Lackland Air Force Base in San Antonio and the remaining time at the Naval Air Station in Belle Chasse).

The pastor at St. Charles during this time was Dr. Myron Madden, an outstanding speaker and pastor. Just after I arrived back in New Orleans, St. Charles held a week-long series of services led by Dr. G. Avery Lee, who was pastor of First Baptist Church in Ruston. It was during this week that I made the decision to transfer my membership from Coliseum Place to St. Charles.

A year later (September 1959), I entered Tulane Law School and began that three-year program.

I began my third year of Law School in September 1961, still very much involved in the College Department activities at St. Charles Ave. Baptist. Returning students and new students were arriving for the Fall Semester at the local colleges and nursing schools. Among the new faces in Training Union on the night of September 17, a beautiful young lady with sparkling brown eyes and sweet smile caught my eye. At the end of the worship service that night, she was among the group of students transferring church membership to St. Charles. Our *new* Pastor, Dr. G. Avery Lee, introduced her as "Barbara Lee, from the First Baptist Church of Clinton, Mississippi." Eagerly joining other church members in line to "extend the hand of Christian fellowship" to the newcomers, I recall asking Barbara if she knew Norman and Marleen Gough, who had recently moved to Mississippi College in Clinton (she did not).

Sometime during the week, I phoned her at the Park View Guest House, where she roomed, and asked her to go with me to the Tulane-Florida football game on October 6. Though she did not know much about football, she accepted. So, on our first date, we witnessed Florida defeat Tulane, 14-3. That was the first of many, many losses by the Green Wave we endured through the years. On one of our early dates, we attended a concert by the world-renowned pianist, Van Cliburn. He played a long series of unrecognized classical pieces, then he stopped playing and left the stage. Assuming the concert to be over at long last, we started to exit the auditorium. As we left the building, we realized that it was only intermission. We did not go back in! We have laughed about this incident a lot of times during the last forty-nine years.

Looking back, it's clear we understood early on that God had aligned circumstances to bring us into each other's lives. When Barbara came back from Dundee after the Thanksgiving break, we became engaged. On March 3, I gave her an engagement ring, which she still wears alongside the matching wedding band. We set a wedding date for July 1, 1962, one month after my graduation from Tulane Law School. The wedding ceremony was in her home church, Dundee Baptist Church (Dundee, Mississippi). I began work at my new job with the Internal Revenue Service in a Federal Building downtown. Barbara completed her final year in Graduate Classical Languages (Latin) during the 1962-63 school year.

We lived in an apartment on South Carrollton Avenue, not far from both Tulane and the church. St. Charles Ave. Church was a vital part of our early married life: we taught High School Sunday School classes, Barbara was active in the W.M.U. (Women's Missionary Union), and we were part of an active Young Couples Training Union group. In early 1963, I was ordained as a deacon at the age of 26.

We bought our first home, far out in Jefferson Parish near the airport, in 1964, but continued to travel back to all services at St. Charles Ave. Baptist Church. Becky was born in 1965 and was enrolled in our church Nursery Department. After Bert's birth in 1968, it became increasingly difficult to travel back and forth to St. Charles to participate in all the church activities. Sadly, and after much prayer and deliberation, we transferred our membership in 1969 to nearby First Baptist Church in Kenner. But, we still cherish those years at St. Charles and are ever mindful of the encouragement and nurturing we received from "the Saints who are at St. Charles."

Jungian Jambalaya

By the end of March 2006, I was still wrestling with my own unexpected emotional grief caused by Hurricane Katrina. As part of my own way of processing—and in dealing with my re-connecting with old friends and neighbors from my youth—I again found journaling essential to my healing.

This private journal entry was soon edited into a musing and published online. It was intended to be included in one of my previous books of musings, but I removed it at the last minute to save for another time . . . a time such as this.

Jungian: ***(adj)*** of or pertaining to the thought and or tradition of psychologist Carl Jung

Carl Jung: early 20th Century psychologist; leader in dream analysis and the belief that the core of the human psyche is spiritual/religious

Jambalaya: ***(n)*** a Creole/Cajun rice dish in which just about anything and everything can be added and stirred to make a meal

Jungian Jambalaya: the title of this reflection

At the end of August 2005, I was living in northern Kentucky. At the end of August 2005, I was about twenty years out of high school and about twenty years out of Louisiana. But at the end of August 2005 (and in the months that followed), time and space disappeared into the mystic.

By early spring 2006, I had almost completely shut down. Shut down at the seminary where I was studying; shut down at the church I was serving; shut down at home.

From the time Hurricane Katrina struck the Gulf Coast and during the five-to-six months that followed—even though I was way up north between Louisville, Kentucky, and Cincinnati, Ohio—I was caught in some transcendent lasso, which was pulling me back to my high school. Back to Destrehan, Louisiana.

I couldn't stop thinking about school experiences (the great ones, the good ones, and the awful ones). I couldn't stop thinking about teachers, classes, specific lessons, band events and practices, and specific people. My body was in Henry County, Kentucky, but I was walking along the roads in Destrehan; I was walking along the levee and looking out over the mighty Mississippi River. I could smell the river, the food, the sweaty gym locker room at school, the sanctuary at the First Baptist Church of Norco, and all the scents in my own house on Ormond Oaks.

Repeatedly, my dreams at night were about Destrehan and New Orleans. School friends from the early/mid 1980s were mixed together with my seminary studies, with my church, and with my family in 2005-2006. It was as if time ceased to exist and everything and everybody were all stirred in together in one big kettle of some sort of Jungian jambalaya.

I obsessively began seeking to locate and reconnect with old neighbors and friends and to establish more frequent contact with the few friends with whom I never lost touch. Thank you letters were sent to a handful of teachers who were tremendously influential in my life; teachers like Mrs. Chaisson and Mr. Greene—whom I hadn't seen nor talked to since I walked across the graduation stage—were thanked for their determination to teach me something, even though I didn't always want to learn. Tears were ever-present in the corners of my eyes; my eyelids were levees fighting to hold back a great flood of emotions.

I clearly remember asking, "God, why am I like this? Why the obsession with who I was and where I was over twenty years ago? Why can't I focus on where I am today and who I am today and what I should be doing today?"

The late Trappist monk Thomas Merton writes about trying to be still to let God do some work in one's self. Maybe this was God doing some work in me . . .

I was disconnected with my past. It was as if I had lived two lives—the first eighteen years in Louisiana (up through high school), and then everything since 1986 when my family moved to Tennessee, and I went off to college, got married, had kids, etc. Maybe God was making whole this divided, schizophrenic self.

I do know that since Katrina, I have never felt more connected to New Orleans, to the River Parishes, and to Louisiana; and thanks to Facebook, I have reconnected with so many people who were very important to me in my younger days, and who directly shaped who I am today.

It's been several years since Hurricane Katrina. Time and space have long since reemerged into the very real present. And thanks be to God, my reality is no longer divided into two seemingly unconnected pieces, but all stirred together into a whole, healthy body of gumbo.

Katrina, with Popcorn

When I first re-connected with Laura Grider (now Laura Hansen) via Facebook, it was several months after Katrina. I hadn't heard from her since I graduated and moved away. I immediately asked her about Katrina, and after she told me a few things, I realized her story needed to be told. I asked her some questions, let her respond, and wrote a musing about her experiences. "Riding Out the Storm (Katrina, with Popcorn)" was included in my second book, Psychic Pancakes & Communion Pizza. *This is my telling of her story.*

And again, because of its relevance to this collection, Smyth & Helwys Publishing graciously granted permission to include it here.

Back in August 2005, I was at home with my wife and sons, sleeping in my bed, and going on with the routines of my life up in Kentucky. At the same time, Hurricane Katrina was destroying the Gulf Coast, levees were breaking, and water was inundating the city of my birth. My best friends from high school down in St. Charles Parish were forced to scatter; I learned later that some were in Florida, many had gone to Texas, and others into the Midwest.

Back in August 2005, while my life was going on as normal and while many of my friends were living in exile, Laura Grider Hansen was riding the storm out—and then the ensuing chaos—on the fifth floor of East Jefferson General Hospital in Metairie.

Popcorn—I always called Laura "Popcorn" because she went to our prom with my best friend, nicknamed "Peanut" (*think of Cracker Jack*)—is a nurse and had been for ten years when Katrina's winds began to blow. Her husband and children packed and left for Houston; Popcorn packed and left to spend an expected two days—at the *most*—working and living at the hospital.

The hurricane passed over—not a direct hit on the New Orleans area. Still, trees were down, roofs were damaged, hotels and offices had windows blown out. For many people in Louisiana, this was to be expected: "No big deal," Popcorn thought. "All fixable."

Of course, the electricity was out. A battery-powered radio served as the voice of the outside world to those inside East Jefferson Hospital, and the reports weren't good. Levees were failing. Water flowed through streets and overflowed the canals around the hospital, and soon reached the tops of houses. The hospital's backup power kept the most necessary equipment working (i.e. vents, pumps, etc.). Popcorn and her colleagues were caring for patients using flashlights and wearing headbands with lights on them. Air conditioning—even in August—was deemed a "non-essential luxury" and was lost halfway through the first full day.

Twelve-hour shifts for twelve straight days. Air mattresses. Six nurses sharing an empty room.

"The radio and news broadcasts that everyone outside of New Orleans was seeing were very true: New Orleans was a War Zone," Popcorn told me. "Although we did not have a lot of trouble at East Jefferson, we were still kept under lock and key and only allowed to move about in the parking garage." The National Guard made hourly rounds on the unit to make sure everything was okay. They (the Guard) were "a pleasure to have around; they made you feel safe and secure when everything else around us was not."

Popcorn and her colleagues befriended a couple of Guardsmen, and those men took the nurses out through the streets near City Park. Riding in military vehicles, Popcorn helped deliver water, food, diapers, baby formula, ice, and personal hygiene supplies to anyone who needed them.

Twelve—not two, but *twelve*—days later, she was able to go home and rest. While her husband and children were still in Houston, Popcorn went to her parents' house in LaPlace—they had just returned home a couple of days earlier. "I was just so exhausted and mentally drained . . . I passed out on their sofa until noon the next day."

As for Popcorn's own damages—there were trees down, one fell onto her son's upstairs bedroom; some roof and other property damage, but "nothing that couldn't be repaired." After two weeks, her family returned home, only to have to evacuate again a couple of weeks later; "and yep," she said, "I was back in gear heading to the hospital for Hurricane Rita."

Popcorn is reflective: “If it had not been for the wonderful group of staff members I worked with, it would have been very different. We laughed and cried together—sometimes at the same time. We all had our moments of weakness; I truly missed my family, dog, my own bed.”

Laura was a “cute little freshman” band member when we met during my senior year. Twenty-plus years later and still stuck with the nickname “Popcorn” (at least as far as I am concerned), she’s now a hero who inspires me. Thanks be to God for Popcorn and all the others who, like her, willingly devote their lives to truly caring for others.

PART TWO

Hurricane Katrina Experiences

(Others' Stories)

Stephanie Hymel Ledet

Stephanie and I met at the beginning of our tenth-grade year at Destrehan High School. I had just transferred in from John Curtis School. Stephanie and I became fast friends in our classes—and we had almost all of our classes together for the next three years. She was my lab partner in Mrs. Bourgeois' tenth-grade biology class—she could handle cutting open the frog we were dissecting; I just tried not to get nauseated. So she cut and I observed (sort of).

When she married in 1996, Stephanie left Destrehan and moved to Kenner, where she and her family still live today.

The week before the storm I talked to my sisters, "What are we going to do? Are we going to go anywhere?" Just minor conversations back and forth. At school, we took precautions; "Okay, put your computers on your desk." But it was like any other hurricane that ever came—you know, you pack three days worth of clothes and you get your important papers together. And it wasn't until the night before we left that things really hit us.

My husband, Clay, had to stay (he works for the pumping stations), so the plan was I was going to take Clay Jr. and the dog we had at the time and go wherever my sister and brother-in-law went. That was just our basic plan. I always plan to leave, but we never go any further than Baton Rouge. In fact, that is where we ended up.

The funny thing is, the night before we left . . . I've never had a more intimate relationship with my husband or my God at that time because we actually lay next to each other holding hands, and we prayed. We are practicing Catholics, but we are not a prayerful couple, if that makes sense? We just lay there holding hands, and we prayed all night until we fell asleep.

We went to Baton Rouge. Clay was at home . . . and he was just going back and forth to work like normal. When they said the storm was coming in closer and it was going to be a big one, they planned to evacuate him. He calls me that night, "I'm in Baton Rouge." He says, "I'm being sent to St. Francisville." And then he'd call like an hour later, "I'm in a Winn Dixie parking lot." Then, he'd call me later. So they never knew where they were going to be. The last time I talked to him, he was at a high school in Franklinton (across the lake). He was at a high school there, and it was raining *inside* the building. So, the last I talked to him was just before the storm hit and he told me he was in Franklinton, and he said, "As soon as the storm passes they are bringing us home." I said, "Okay."

When they are showing the levees breaking, I'm thinking, "Those poor people . . . They're going to lose everything." Then . . . there is a reporter at the front of Loyola—and he's talking, and he's pointing down the street, and he's saying, "We can't even get in, and rumors are the water is to the rooftops." When I saw that, that's when I just kind of crumbled; I'm like, "Wait a minute, I'm thinking 'poor people' in other places . . . I just became a 'poor people.'" It turned out luckily that it wasn't up to the roof, but it was bad enough—we had two-and-a-half feet of water.

We only stayed in Baton Rouge about three or four days, then we came back to my sister's house in Norco. They had no electricity, but we had generators. My brother-in-law worked in Gonzales so he was still able to go back and forth to work.

It was a total of eleven days that I couldn't reach my husband—couldn't talk to him, didn't know where he was, or if he was okay. And then, what ends up happening, it was just really freaky. I didn't know how to text, and neither did he. My sister would text him, and it would be a day, and then he would text back. But because he didn't know how to text, he would just say, "I'm fine," or something like that . . . I took my son driving, and right by the Norco refinery there is a big cell tower. I pulled right up under the cell tower, and I was able to get my husband. So, I'm talking to him, and I'm crying buckets; and my son is sitting there, and he's shaking, and he's talking to his dad. Well, all of a sudden some cell tower people pull up, and they're like, "Ma'am, you can't be here, and you need to move." I just lost it. I turned around and said, "I have not spoken to my husband in eleven days. This boy doesn't even know that his father is alive. I'm not leaving because I got a connection." And they said, "Ma'am, take all the time you need." They sat in their trucks and waited while we sat there and talked to him. So, we were able to talk to him, but I still hadn't seen him.

My brother-in-law, Greg, and my other brother-in-law (who was just my sister's boyfriend at the time) drove me to the first pump station that's back here and we just took back roads and kind of snuck our way in. There were dead fish, I guess from the lake, all over the road. We make it to that pump station—Clay is not there. "I think he's at such and such," so we went to *that* pump station. He's not there. Well, then, it was getting dark. We had to go back home because there were no street lights or anything, and it was really creepy to be out at night. So, the next day we go and we hit West Esplanade—you'd have to drive a little bit on one side and then you'd have to find a cross street and get on the other side and drive the wrong way because trees and power lines were all over. It was just a horrible scene. We get to the pump station and, I keep saying it was like *An Officer and a Gentleman*—you know, when he walks into the factory? I'm running through the station. I'm going up and down. I'm looking all over for him. I run outside . . . Clay is just standing there outside on the deck looking at the lake. I just start screaming. He comes running over. We're hugging. My two brothers-in-law—big, bulky guys—when I turn around, both of them are crying. You know, it was just very emotional.

We ended up staying with my sister in Norco; her family of four and my family. We stayed with them for eight months. We lived in their son's bedroom—they moved their son out, so we had two single beds. Clay and I were in one; little Clay in the other. That's how we lived for eight months.

The FEMA trailer came rather quickly. I want to say that within a month we had a trailer. My father-in-law lives with us, and he's in his eighties. The first night in the FEMA trailer Paw Paw falls and hurts himself; my husband is six-feet two-inches, and he can't fit in the shower. It was goofy stuff. We went back to my sister—"Okay, can we please just stay?" So, we ended up using the trailer more as a place to cool off, a place to use the bathroom, a place to clean up while working on our house. We were lucky in the sense that we didn't have to live in it.

I can't listen to the Police anymore. The whole time we were fixing the house—we had a stereo that made it through; it had the CD of the Police stuck in it—all we ever heard was "Roxanne" and "Message in a Bottle." We were excited to have something, you know . . . but I can't listen to them anymore. And I love them . . . can't even listen to Sting anymore.

I really don't know how to put this—when you get home, and you have to clear everything out, and you start thinking, "I lost this, and I don't have this anymore," and you start looking at all the things . . . Then you look around and say, "But I have my family. We are going to be okay. We can do it." And it makes you closer. It makes you appreciate things a lot more.

Debbie Induni

Debbie has been in my most inner-circle of Destrehan High friends almost since I arrived there in 1983; she is one of the few people I have remained in contact with (though, admittedly, sporadically) since our high school days. She hung out with us sometimes, and when she wasn't with us, we'd take her leftover pizza—usually knocking on her window sometime after midnight. She put up with a lot of our nonsense, and that alone speaks volumes about her character.

Over the years our individual journeys have taken each of us far, far away from Destrehan. Debbie lived in the River Parishes for about twelve years; then after high school, she moved "here and there." She lived outside of Louisiana for sixteen years after graduation; living in Allen, Texas (a suburb of Dallas), at the time of Katrina. In 2006, she and her children returned to St. Charles Parish, and she once again calls Destrehan her home.

Leading up to Katrina I was hearing a lot of conflicting news from our local stations who were making it "the storm to end all storms." My family and friends were much less anxious about the fierceness of the storm—they are well-versed in hurricanes and only worry when it is time to worry. My initial thoughts were "I will worry when it is time to worry," and "oh no, if they evacuate they are coming here!"

As Katrina approached and the evacuations started, it was very apparent that, despite the damage the storm would do, the mishandling and degradation that it would impose on many of the evacuees would leave scars worse than the storm.

I housed my mom, step-dad, sister-in-law, niece, and various pets for about one-to-two weeks.

When Katrina became a reality, it was jaw-dropping to stand on the "outside" and have life be in complete normalcy, while so much tragedy was occurring in my hometown. I remember going shopping with my mom the day Katrina hit, and Dallas was moving along just as always—and I just stood there thinking, "people are axing their way out of roofs, drowning, etc., and I am shopping like normal." It was much like the sensation when 9/11 occurred.

After Katrina moved out, my brother—who had to stay and work at Ochsner Hospital—was feeding us "insider" reports, so we knew our neck of the woods did not have much devastation. The hospital had armed guards surrounding it, due to armed looters. I remember just feeling very helpless and sad.

I heard some people referring to the disaster as some sort of "ethnic cleansing" for the city. I have never seen people and all forms of government take such a matter-of-fact attitude towards the suffering of others. I was mortified by the jokes and comments I heard about their hopes that a whiter version of New Orleans would be developed after the storm.

We maintained contact, of course, with all of our friends that evacuated and also with my brother until right after Katrina passed over—at that point, we lost contact with him for about two days.

I returned to live in Destrehan one year after Katrina, and I was truly saddened for the city of New Orleans. The city was such huge part of my teenage life. Even at that age I loved the atmosphere of the city. I loved its downtrodden agedness, its essence of history, the diverse population, the riverboat jazz cruises, walks on the moonwalk, the French Market, the Saenger Theatre, etc. They were my most beautiful memories, and I would never be able revisit them. My first drive down Canal Street was an emotional mix of loss, sadness, anger.

Now that I am in the insurance industry here, I hear horror stories everyday from New Orleans residents. These people who are *finally*—in 2010—rebuilding their lives, their credit, buying new homes, trying to recover from the total material losses they incurred from Miss Katrina . . . but as I suspected, the emotional scars will never heal.

Marta Gieseler Wootan

Marta was an energetic freshman flute player in the DHS band when I was a junior. During my last two years of high school, I can't remember when she wasn't a part of my core group of friends who were always hanging out together. Less than a month before my family moved to Tennessee, Marta was my date for the senior prom.

Marta is not a native of the River Parishes. In fact, before she was seven years old, she lived several places—from Chicago to California, up to Washington, down to Utah, and eventually landing in Destrehan, Louisiana. Overall, though, she has lived in the region about twenty-two years; she now lives in a new house she and her husband built in Montz, right on the edge of St. Charles Parish. They had the land and were getting ready to build when Katrina showed up and put everything on hold. At that time, they were living in Destrehan.

So many of us were thinking we could ride this one out. The older folks said if they could get through Hurricanes Betsy and Camille they could get through anything—it was never supposed to get worse than those two. Margaret Orr, our local meteorologist, was the only one showing true concern. We just watched and waited. I was hoping that this was going to be like the last one I rode out . . . not a big deal at all.

But, it was just such a *huge* storm. When it was in the middle of the Gulf, it covered the entire body of water. So, I thought I should at least go to my mother-in-law's house in Baker, Louisiana (in East Baton Rouge Parish), just to get Drew (my son) to a place where it wouldn't be so scary. Still, though, just thinking a lot of wind, a lot of rain, and the power would go out.

My grandfather had a major stroke and was declared brain-dead a week before the storm. His body was still living in a hospice in Denver; my father was already there to be with him. So, we had plane tickets to get out of town, but the intention was not evacuation—just to go be with our family and eventually have a funeral. Our flight was the first one to be canceled the Saturday before the storm hit. That is when we started using the term "evacuate;" that is when the urgency kicked in. We were planning to leave anyway . . . but then it became evident that we *had* to.

I was so worried about being stuck in the nightmarish traffic—the previous threat (Ivan, I think) put people on the road for *seventeen* hours just to get to Baton Rouge. "Please, God, don't let us get stuck in traffic, run out of gas, and get hit by the hurricane in the car." That's all I could think.

I kick into full-on planning and organizing mode in stressful situations, which takes the "feeling" out of it. Logistics are much easier to work through when you aren't afraid—it's just a coping mechanism. Since my father wasn't there, I also had to keep calm so my mother wouldn't lose it (planning and organizing doesn't comfort her like it does me).

We packed a few precious items (photos and the like), but didn't have to worry much about clothes. Whatever we didn't have, we could get from my grandfather's clothing store. We packed toys and books for Drew in the car. My husband, Kurt, took our three dogs to stay at his brother's house in Baton Rouge. Kurt did not want to leave his three daughters, who also live in Baton Rouge. As much as I hated to be separated from him, I knew he had to stay.

It took us ten hours to drive to Houston to catch our flight to Denver—there we stayed at my aunt's house. We spent every waking moment in the hospice with my grandfather after that.

I remember the morning after we thought the storm had passed and that we (the New Orleans area) came out of it okay. My father burst into my room to wake me up by saying "New Orleans is going underwater!" I jumped out of bed and ran to the TV. I couldn't believe it. The news helicopter was flying over streets I drove on everyday. But you couldn't see streets . . . only water and roofs. We spent the rest of the days in my grandfather's room watching the TV for any sign that our houses were okay.

All those people stuck on the roofs . . . the abandoned animals . . . the floating bodies . . . Why wasn't anyone helping them? Why were those people still stuck at the Convention Center and at the Dome? When was someone going to help them?

Our government's lack of response still bewilders me, and it is the main reason why you will never consider me a fan of George W. Bush. No, "Brownie" did *not* do a great job! It was almost unbearable.

Once word spread around the hospice that we were from New Orleans, those nurses spent just as much time taking care of us as they did of their patients. Then we had to plan and attend my grandfather's funeral. The nurses and doctors told us my grandfather had his stroke and died because he knew coming to be with him would get us out of harm's way—I didn't find comfort in that. I wanted him to wake up.

I wasn't able to talk to Kurt for two-and-a-half weeks. I got in touch with his brother, so I knew he was okay. But, not being able to reach Kurt was tough. All my cousins and extended family were on e-mail, so we were able to keep up with them.

I was gone from Destrehan for three weeks. Returning home was very disorienting. The trees were all sideways. There was nobody on the road. It was beyond quiet in my neighborhood—it was like a ghost town.

We were so happy to be home . . . so what did we want to do? Go out and eat—that's what we do here, right? But where do you go . . . nothing is open . . . no one is here.

The power was back on by the time I returned. A tree had fallen on our mailbox, but everything else was okay. Kurt had been home within five days of the storm's passing, so he had the yards and refrigerators cleaned up already.

My job was still there simply because I am lucky enough to work for the only New Orleans hospital that didn't close. Ochsner is located on the very edge of the city line, and the water got really close to coming into the building, but it didn't.

These days we're totally back to normal. We put off building our new house (we were scheduled to start in October 2006). We knew we had to let all the available labor and materials go to people who *had* to *rebuild*. But, that is done now—we're in our new house.

The occasional drive through Slidell or to the Ninth Ward still shocks me . . . they are still where they were the day after.

Billy Riecke

Billy is one-half of the infamous Riecke brothers from the Destrehan High School Band. Very innovative, hilariously cynical, and unapologetically geeky, Billy, his brother Chris, and their good friend Kiley were brilliantly disruptive in a morale-boosting way that made my senior year of band not only more fun and memorable, but also that made us want to perform better together. Even "Mr. Cat"—our band director—appreciated their antics.

When I moved to Tennessee, I received a homemade video (back in the days of huge clunky VHS cameras) from the Riecke Brothers. They devised an entire storyline and filmed a movie about Mr. Catalano's legendary pointed-toe boots . . . and a cockroach. My copy wore out years ago. It was true genius in its absurd simplicity.

Billy has always lived in the New Orleans area. Raised in the River Parishes, he eventually moved out to, as he put it, "the bustling suburbs of Jefferson Parish" when he was in his twenties. In 2003, he and his wife, Susan, bought their first house—in Metairie. In August 2005, Susan was a respiratory therapist at East Jefferson General Hospital, and Billy worked for Southern Rehab, a company that specialized in providing medical equipment for patients with special needs (mostly wheelchairs).

The summer of 2005 had been an unusually active hurricane season, so when we heard about another hurricane headed toward the Gulf of Mexico, we were cautious, but given the forecast track, not overly concerned. Most of the forecast models had predicted the storm to make landfall in Florida, *not* Louisiana. That Friday before the storm, I was delivering a hospital bed to a patient's house when I saw the news report on their television—Katrina had failed to make the predicted northerly turn, and was on a direct course for New Orleans.

Within minutes of seeing that report, my cell phone rang. It was my mother. She told me that she had already made reservations at a hotel in Natchitoches, Louisiana. She wanted to know if Susan and I would want to evacuate with them, along with my brother and his family. I told her I'd have to call her back.

When I got home that evening, I had the most difficult conversation I have ever had with my wife. Around the same time I got the call from my mom, Susan was asked to work at the hospital through the duration of the storm. While I didn't want to leave her, I knew the hospital would be one of the safest places around. So we made our plans. She would pack up a few day's worth of clothes, some creature comforts, and some snack food, and spend what we thought would only be the weekend in the hospital. I would pack up our most irreplaceable possessions (pictures, documents, etc.) and our dog, Buster, and "head for the hills," so to speak.

We spent all day Saturday making plans, getting our contact lists together, and packing. I was leaving around 1:30 the next morning (Sunday), and she was reporting to work a few hours later. That evening, we sat in our backyard and enjoyed the sunset. It was abnormally pleasant for an August evening. The air was warm and dry, not the usual humid steam bath that is New Orleans. As we watched Buster chase squirrels around the backyard, we sat silent, just holding hands. Although we didn't say anything, we both knew this could very well be the last time we had a backyard to enjoy. We got a few hours of sleep, and when 1:30 in the morning came around, we said our tearful goodbyes.

About thirty minutes later, I was at my brother's house in Montz, a small town along the Mississippi River. There, along with my brother and his wife and kids, were my parents and my grandparents. A short while later, we were all on the road heading north. My family always liked traveling at night, because there was less traffic and aggravation. This habit had proved quite fortunate for us this time. Even though the contra-flow evacuation was in effect, the cars were all moving at the speed limit. We made it to Natchitoches a few hours later, and we waited a few more hours in the parking lot until our rooms were ready.

That evening, like everybody else, we were transfixed around the television. We watched the news reports about the highways and interstates jammed solid with evacuees. We saw the forecast track of a powerful storm with a bulls-eye on New Orleans. Whenever I could, I tried calling Susan.

Sometimes I could get through, but more often than not, the circuits were jammed. She told me she was fine, and that there were plenty of police and other emergency workers staying at the hospital (a few years prior, I had worked at East Jefferson, too; I knew they had a massive generator system, and had their own well for water). Susan said that there were a lot of people there—mainly employees and their immediate family members—but everybody was fine. The storm was going to hit between sometime that night and into the early morning hours.

That was the last decent night's sleep I got for quite a while.

When I woke up the next morning, the TV news (as it had been all night) was on. Yes, Katrina did make landfall. Yes, there was some damage, but nothing major. The experts at the National Weather Service estimated that she lost some of her punch and was about a category three when she made landfall. Reporters were in the streets of New Orleans, in the early morning hours, reporting that the worst had passed.

Or so they thought.

Suddenly water started filling the streets. Places that had no noticeable rainfall accumulation were now starting to fill with brackish water. Then, the reports started coming in: Levees had breached; not just one or two, but LOTS of them. It seemed all of my family members were perched on the edge of a hotel bed, watching the aerial shots of all the flooding and the breaches. I think we were in a state of shock for the first few minutes.

Then it hit us like a ton of bricks. My mind started racing. I thought, "Well, if this is happening all over New Orleans, what's happening just eight miles away at my house in Metairie?"

I tried all morning to get in touch with Susan, but I got the now familiar drone—*all circuits are busy, please try again.* I was flipping channels between CNN, Fox News, and MSNBC—looking for any reports or any aerial shots of Metairie. About an hour later, I had flipped to a station that was showing a house on fire, while it was surrounded by what appeared to be three feet of water. After a few minutes, the camera on the helicopter panned up, and there it was—East Jefferson General Hospital. Where my wife was staying. Only four miles from my house. Under water.

That's when I can safely say I lost it. My first and only instinct was to grab a bottle of Bacardi 151 rum that I had packed along for the trip, and I started drinking. My nephew asked me, "Uncle Billy, why are you drinking?"

I don't quite remember saying it, but he told me later that I responded, "Because I don't want to remember any of this."

In between the short bouts of sobriety over the next couple of hours, we were hearing stories of gangs invading hospitals in order to steal the drugs, and hospital patients and staff having to be evacuated by army helicopters. Sober or intoxicated, I still tried to call Susan every hour or so. Finally, later that night, I got through. The call only lasted a few seconds, but those fleeting moments seemed like an eternity. Susan said that they were safe, and that the army and police were using East Jefferson as a sort of "base camp." They were running off generators, but had food and water. I told her I would come back as soon as I could, then the line went dead.

At that moment, I realized what was really important in life. I no longer cared if my house was destroyed, and that we might have lost all of our material possessions. All that mattered was that my wife was safe.

The next day, my brother got word that his neighbors had gone back to their house in Montz, and they had running water; there was no electricity, but it was dry and safe there. We decided to get back as soon as we could. Wasting no time, we packed the cars and hit the road. Along the way, my brother picked up a generator at a Home Depot. Because we got a head start, we made it back in a few hours. Because they (military, state police, etc.) were not letting anybody back into the New Orleans area, I stayed at my brother's house with the rest of my family for a few days. We were cramped and hot, but we were together. And safe.

Over the next few days I was able to get in touch with Susan more often as the phone lines and cell phone towers were being repaired. She said she heard that all of Metairie had been flooded, but she said that it was still a rumor. Then, on the Friday following the storm, they started letting people back into Jefferson Parish to just "check on their property," but had to leave that evening. Well, I hopped in my van . . .

When I got back into Jefferson Parish, the first thing I noticed was the power lines all over the largely abandoned highways. The next thing that hit me was that there were hardly any trees left standing. As I navigated the streets, I made a detour to my house, just to see what was left. To my amazement, it had survived. The flood waters barely came up to my slab. There was debris everywhere. I walked around back, noticing all the shingles and siding that had been torn off by the wind. My back yard was a complete mess, and the fences had been blown down, but it was still intact. I pried the plywood off of the front door and made my way inside. That's when I found the most unexpected thing—we had electricity and cable!

After securing the front door again, I headed for the East Jefferson Hospital. Driving down Veterans Boulevard was surreal to say the least. It was the time of day that should have been morning rush hour, and I was the only person on the road. I had to go through three separate checkpoints to get to the hospital. The first were paramedics armed with shotguns, the second were Jefferson Parish Deputies armed with pistols and semi-automatic rifles. The final checkpoint was staffed by National Guardsmen armed with machine guns. That's when I really knew Susan was in good hands. I went to what I guess was a makeshift information desk. They paged Susan for me. After what seemed like hours, but in fact was only three minutes, I saw my wife.

We stayed locked in each other's arms and cried like babies. People watched, but we were oblivious. I told her the house was relatively fine and gave her a garbage bag full of clean clothes that she had asked for (all of our luggage was already in use). We had a limited time together because she was technically "on duty" and had to finish making her rounds. I told her I was staying at my brother's house but would try to get back home as soon as I could. Later that evening, as soon as I got back to my brother's place, I packed my van. It was announced that Jefferson Parish wasn't letting anybody back in until further notice, but I was never one to really follow the rules.

The next morning, I left my brother's house around 4:30 a.m., hoping the local authorities would still be catching some much needed shut-eye. I stayed on River Road, hoping a "back way" into the city would be less likely to be guarded. As I approached the parish line, I was getting nervous. But when the "Welcome to Jefferson Parish" sign came and went without a single roadblock or cop car, I breathed a sigh of relief. Snaking through the back streets of Kenner and Metairie, I made it home. Buster, my faithful mutt, was almost excited as I was to be back in familiar territory.

The following week was spent cleaning up debris, trying to get my fences back upright, and basically trying to keep watch over my neighborhood. I was the only person on the block. Amid all the stories of looting and roving gangs, I was pleasantly surprised to see the National Guardsmen on foot patrol. FEMA finally got its act together and started delivering MREs, water, and ice. Each morning I would drive down to "the depot" (basically a glorified road block about a mile away) and get my supplies. Susan would still be at the hospital for a few more days, and I found myself going stir crazy. My in-laws lived just a few streets over, so I went and started cleaning up their yard and cutting the grass (it was still August, and if you don't stay on top of that St. Augustine, it can get out of hand real easy). So they got some free lawn maintenance. Susan's grandmother and uncle each had houses on the same block, so they also got the treatment.

A few days later, my boss called to check up on me. He informed me that our shop had about eighteen inches of water, and a lot of our power wheelchairs were ruined. Also, he had been getting calls from some of our patients wanting to know if we were open and able to repair wheelchairs. So, bright and early the next morning, Southern Rehab was open for business. We still didn't have power at the shop, so we worked out in the parking lot. In between gutting all the sheet rock and moldy carpeting, we would repair flat tires, adjust seats, and try to get the motors running on our wheelchair-bound patients. I don't think we even charged them.

Susan returned home the next day after I started back to work, and life became a little more normal—although it would never truly be the same. About a week later the waters finally started to go down in New Orleans and in the neighboring community of Chalmette. My boss got a call from one of his patients—the patient's insurance company would not provide a new wheelchair unless he could prove his old one was destroyed in the hurricane. So, off we were, on a mission.

Aside from being a rehab therapist, my boss was also a volunteer Orleans Parish deputy sheriff. That proved to be quite useful, because it got us past the security blockade at the Orleans Parish line. Our first stop on the "Magical Misery Tour," as I have now started to call it, was Children's Hospital. Children's Hospital is located just a block or two from the Mississippi River, which means it didn't flood. My boss thought that maybe if there were some staff there, that they would let us take some wheelchair parts to use for some of the patients who were on their way back home. Well, instead of being met by staff members, we had two army guys point machine guns at our heads. After some quick explaining, they simply told us to "turn around and don't come back." You don't argue when there is a machine gun pointed at your head.

So, we continued on to Chalmette, which is located in the adjoining parish of St. Bernard. When most of the country hears about the flooding of New Orleans during Hurricane Katrina, they really only hear about "The Ninth Ward." That was indeed horrible and devastating, but there were also other places totally decimated—like the *entire* St. Bernard Parish. As we made our way further into Chalmette, it looked more like an alien planet than anything I had ever seen pre-Katrina. There was no color. Everything was covered in a grayish-brownish layer of dried muck. Only the sky provided any clue that we weren't in some monochromatic alternate universe. So much mud had been washed in that you could not tell where the streets were located, since houses had floated off of their slabs in all directions.

The ground had become dried and cracked. Every once in a while, we'd find a signpost still intact, and try to match it up with our trusty Rand-McNally. No GPS for us—we're hardcore like that.

A few wrong turns and a couple of detours around shrimping boats straddling the road, and we found what was left of our patient's house. We were informed that the chair was left in his van, which was *supposed* to be in his driveway. Of course, it wasn't. It had washed across where the street had been, and wedged itself between two trees in what had been a patch of woods. It now looked like the surface of Mars with a couple of giant black spears stuck in the ground. With the help of a crowbar and hammer, we got the side door of the van open, and took a picture of what was left of the wheelchair. I had never seen stalactites and stalagmites made of mud before, but inside of a Chevy van and after the storm . . . anything was possible. The picture was sent to the insurance company with the accompanying message, "I don't know if you knew this, but we've had a little bit of trouble here. You may want to watch the news once in a while."

As time went on, life started getting less crazy. I can't use the word "normal," because normal implies that things are getting back the way they used to be. We've all accepted the hard fact that things will not ever get back to the way they used to be. But in this less-crazy world, there were things that kept surprising us. Little things, we found, gave us so much joy—like a grocery store re-opening. Being able to get fresh fruit again. Seeing more friends and family come back. Finding out that while some of our favorite places had been lost forever, a few actually survived. And, I practically cried the day I found out Hubig's Pies were being made again.

From then on, we've learned some pretty important lessons:

1. Material possessions mean nothing. Sure, they're cool and all, but when it comes down to it, you'd give them all up in a heartbeat just to know your loved ones are safe.

2. You are only supposed to eat one MRE a day, not one for each meal. Those things are something like 2000 calories each, and there's a reason that they come with little laxatives.

3. If you're going to plant a tree around New Orleans, it better either be an Oak or a Cypress. Nothing else will ever survive.

4. Never, EVER, take the National Guard for granted. They did so much around here, and I could never express in words how truly grateful I am for rescuing us, protecting us, and helping us.

5. Have a good shovel. When the sewage treatment plants are down, and you're forbidden by law to flush, you'd better learn how to dig a good latrine.

6. While the National Guard was there, a lot of government agencies weren't. You can't count on anybody to bail you out. You need to be prepared to do it yourself.

7. Nothing brings people closer together than adversity. It's truly amazing how we've rebounded by helping each other, leaning on each other, and loving each other.

8. Hubig's Pies rule.

Chris Riecke

Chris, Billy's younger brother, has always lived in the River Parishes. He grew up in New Sarpy (St. Charles Parish), got married and moved to LaPlace (in neighboring St. John the Baptist Parish), and eventually returned to settle with his family in Montz (back to St. Charles).

About a year-and-a-half before Hurricane Katrina, he built a new house in Montz (described by Chris as a "small community just west of the Spillway; site of a Mississippi River levee break in the 1880s, and of a tragic train accident in November 1912"). That's the kind of stuff Chris has always known. Chris was a freshman during my senior year. The Riecke brothers ensured that my senior year in the DHS band was a complete blast.

We knew a storm was out there, but it was down by the Keys, and it was a measly Category 1 . . . nothing to worry about—just another small storm about to enter the Gulf. At the time, my parents were living with us because their house was being built next door. We were actually joking about the amount of lumber projectiles available within feet of my house (their house was just a framed structure at the time).

But what was funny—the Thursday before the storm, I came home from work, and my mom said she had booked three rooms up in Natchitoches (where they filmed *Steel Magnolias*). I thought, "Okay, Chicken Little, overreacting again!"

My wife and I had NO desire to leave (she loves bad weather anyway). My thoughts? "Still not leaving," and, "look at ALL the IDIOTS out there in the parking lot known as the Interstate system." We had no intentions on leaving, but felt like boarding up the windows might be a wise thing at this point. Really, the only thing I was worried about is that we had just switched homeowners insurance about two months prior to Katrina making landfall, and I was worried that if something were to happen, would they cover it?

Okay . . . then Katrina found the warmest spot in the Gulf and parked herself right over it. She had no intentions of going anywhere, and at the time, neither did we. (Lesson learned: Never have a staring contest with a hurricane). By this time—it was Saturday morning—I had bought the plywood (which there was still plenty of at Home Depot). My dad and I spent a good part of the morning boarding up the windows. My mom had made up her mind that they were going to take my grandparents and evacuate to the hotel where she made her reservations. By this time, Billy, who was wifeless (Susan had to stay at the hospital) had his dog, Buster, in tow. My mom let us know that she would hold the other room for us in the event we changed our minds.

But something happened at about 9:30 that Saturday night. All day long, my wife and I had wrestled with the decision to evacuate. We both wanted to stay, but my concerns were for my kids. At the time Gabrielle was 11 and Austin was 9. I was running "worst case scenarios" through my head: flooding, tornadoes, high winds . . . all disasters of biblical proportions. I could see myself and my wife surviving said disasters in pure Hollywood style. But, as in most Hollywood disaster movies, the weak actors never survive. I felt pretty confident that I could save myself and my wife, but my fear was that I couldn't save them all if we all stayed. With that said, it was planned for the kids to go with my parents (leaving at 4:00 Sunday morning to avoid the traffic), and Dawn and I would stay. But I could tell, though, that she didn't want to be separated from the kids—which brought us to the "What-the-Hell-Do-We-Do-Now?" point.

Again, with everyone in bed early on Saturday night, and the house pitch black from all the windows being boarded up, Dawn and I were in the bed and watching the news—which now had become an around-the-clock media event preaching the end of the world. Then, old horror stories I've heard about Hurricane Andrew started going through my mind—like how one Florida family rode out the storm in a their minivan, inside their garage.

Call it cold feet, paranoia, or whatever, but I made the executive decision to get the hell out of Dodge!!! With the decision made, it was time to get my butt in gear. I was outside all night that Saturday night feverishly throwing lawn furniture and garden gnomes in the shed—reminiscent of the scene in *Close Encounters* where Richard Dreyfus tears up the chicken coop and throws it in his house to make Devils Tower in his living room. Finally at

3:00 a.m., the house was "Katrina-ready," down to the boat being unhooked from its trailer like setting cattle free.

When 4:00 am came around, I was in no shape to drive . . . everyone else got a decent night's sleep. We loaded up all the vehicles, including our pets (except the cat), turned off the gas to the house, and left in the darkness, like a band of gypsies. I tossed and turned, and tried to get some sleep in the front seat of our Ford Escape while Dawn drove.

We stayed at the palatial Best Western of Natchitoches. We got there at about 10:00 Sunday morning, and the hotel was the closest thing to a redneck refugee camp I've ever seen . . . not that I've ever seen one to compare it to. And the best part—the other "undesirable" half of New Sarpy was there. Of all the hotels in the state, these "people" had managed to secure rooms at the same hotel as my family and me. And the leader of this rogue band of imbeciles . . . well let's just say, if New Sarpy had a Village Idiot, this was him! When we were kids, I remember that the woman who birthed this goon would yell his name from the front door of their trailer hourly, like New Sarpy's version of Big Ben. Finally, about noon, we got into our room.

When we woke up the next morning (Monday morning), Katrina was already hitting New Orleans. The only good news is that sometime earlier that morning, it had taken a brief, and I mean very brief, jog to the east, sparing New Orleans from a direct hit. I thought it was cool watching the idiot reporters try to deliver a report in hurricane conditions—I kept waiting for somebody to get hit with a garbage can lid!

The kids thought they were on vacation—with multiple trips to the pool. That says a lot for our vacation selections (I promise it has gotten better).

My thoughts were all about my house, which was less than one-and-a-half years old. But really, at no point did I ever think anything would happen to it. I felt pretty confident that I had left no stone unturned.

All day Monday, I couldn't sit still. It felt like I had to get home—sort of like the feeling that you left the stove on while you're at Walmart. I told Dawn as soon as we get up Tuesday morning, we would head back home to beat roadblocks. And, we did. We made it home Tuesday, the day after the storm, at around 10:00 a.m.

The biggest word on the street was that there was no electricity as far north as Baton Rouge. With that said, we stopped at every Lowe's and Home Depot on the way home in the quest for a generator. Our search was unsuccessful.

What stands out in my mind the most about the drive back is that the scenery resembled a post-apocalyptic film: abandoned cars along the road (left where they ran out of gas), downed trees, downed powerlines and telephone poles . . .

When we got home, to our surprise, the house was still standing. The two big-damage ticket-items were our fence and our flooring. Our wooden fence, which ran 150-feet along the back side of the house, had completely been laid flat. None of the twenty-eight posts, *none of them*, were straight. They all were bent at the first mounting hole. The other item was our wooden floors—the ice-maker had melted (due to the lack of electricity for about a day-and-a-half), and the water sat on our wooden floors and caused them to buckle, and they were eventually replaced.

Since the refinery was shut down and manpower scarce, restarting the plant was not going to be immediate. After fighting to keep a generator fed and taking in three more houseguests, I was ready to go back to work—if anything, just to get air-conditioning. We were without power (other than a small generator that my neighbor found in Baton Rouge) for almost a week. Doesn't sound like much, but for some reason, that was the worst heat I've ever felt in the days after a storm. I remember lying in bed sweating and smelling exhaust fumes from the generator outside. So, needless to say, I was happy to go back to work.

Everybody's fine now, and everything is back to "Riecke-normal." However, three of our surviving troop have passed on: my grandmother, Billy's dog Buster, and the cat we left behind to guard the house (the real Katrina survivor). As a result of so many people losing their houses in St. Bernard Parish, our subdivision went from a few scattered homes to a full-fledged community from all of the "Chalmettians" moving in.

Kiley Anderson

Kiley was one of younger guys in the DHS Band during my senior year. Kiley, along with the Riecke brothers, were the clowns that could crack anybody up at any moment—and you just couldn't be mad at them. I enjoyed getting to know Kiley that year, then I moved away . . . we reconnected via Facebook and have resumed our friendship after over a twenty-year break.

Kiley lived in various Louisiana towns almost all of his life and attended college at LSU. When Katrina passed through, Kiley was living in Prairieville, near Baton Rouge. He has lived in Texas since 2009.

I was working claims in the aftermath of the BP Texas City refinery explosion in Texas City, Texas. Being in the insurance adjusting business, I always watch every hurricane closely, but since I was busy at the time, I didn't watch as closely as I usually do until it became apparent that it was going to hit New Orleans as a Category 4 or 5 hurricane. Then, I really started paying attention. A friend of mine from Eunice, Louisiana, was with me, and we stayed up all night watching the news the night it hit and into the next day when the levees broke. My girlfriend at the time was at my house in Prairieville, and she called every hour or so until her cell phone battery died. The power was out, so she had to plug it into her car to charge it.

At first I just thought this was the same stuff we go through all the time. I was living in Baton Rouge when New Orleans evacuated for Hurricane Georges in 1998; my apartment was right at the "10-12 split" (where Interstates 10 and 12 split), so I could sit on my balcony and watch the thousands of cars stuck in traffic moving at 5 mph through Baton Rouge. I was also working in Metairie when Ivan headed our way; it took me seven hours to get from New Orleans to my house in Baton Rouge during that evacuation. I just thought—like most people—that the city would evacuate, there would be some wind and rain, and everyone would go back home, just like every other time we ran this drill. I didn't house any family, but I had two insurance adjuster friends from Utah who stayed in my extra bedrooms while they worked claims in Baton Rouge and New Orleans.

I've always had a love-hate relationship with New Orleans. I love the history and the culture; I hate the crime and political corruption and the defeatist attitude that many people from the region seem to have. Usually when I thought about New Orleans, it was the bad things that stuck out to me; but watching the city being torn apart on live TV really hit me pretty hard. I kept watching the news and telling my friends, "I used to shop there," "I ate at that restaurant a thousand times," and, "I used to work in that building." It was like a huge part of my own history was being wiped away. I worked in a building in Metairie right on the Jefferson/Orleans Parish line (17th Street Canal). As the rescuers were bringing survivors to the 17th Street Canal bridge on Veterans to unload them, I kept seeing that office in the background. It really hit close to home at that point.

Most of my friends evacuated. My company headquarters was in Metairie, but everyone there had evacuated to Natchez to set up temporary offices to keep things going. My girlfriend was at my house outside of Baton Rouge. She kept me informed and kept her phone charged in her car so I was never really out of contact with anyone.

I had to finish up my work in Texas City before I could head to New Orleans to start helping in the rebuilding there. Ironically, when I was finally able to get out of Texas City, I got caught up in the Galveston/Houston evacuation for Hurricane Rita. Texas wasn't taking any chances and was evacuating five days before Rita hit. The good thing was, once I got onto I-10 it was smooth sailing because while everyone was heading out of coastal Louisiana, I was heading into it.

Once I got back to Baton Rouge after helping out post-Katrina, it had become the largest city in the state—the roads were packed, the grocery stores had mostly empty shelves, gas was hard to find. It was a very different feeling. So much so that after dealing with post-Katrina Baton Rouge for three years, I was happy to move to Dallas/Fort Worth.

Baton Rouge has never been the same since. The small-town feel kind of faded and traffic, which wasn't all that great before, had become unbearable. One of the reasons I liked Baton Rouge so much was that it wasn't anything like New Orleans. After the storm, though, we got all of the problems of New Orleans and none of the charm.

Darla DiGirolamo LeBlanc

I don't remember when I met first Darla or her family. I was ten years old—that much I know for sure, because that's how old I was when we moved to Destrehan and when we started attending the First Baptist Church of Norco. Darla, her sisters, and her parents were active at FBC. Darla's family and my family got along well; being some of the few Tulane Green Wave fans sprinkled among the throngs of LSU Tiger fans, we bonded together in our suffering (and our occasional celebrating). Long after my parents moved my sister and me to West Tennessee, we would bump into Darla's parents at Tulane road games; even after I was married with kids of my own, there was Mr. Nick at the 1998 Liberty Bowl in Memphis cheering along with my parents, my son and me as Tulane went undefeated—a perfect 12-0.

Mr. Nick was 80 years old and still going strong when Katrina hit. He passed away three years later in 2008. Mrs. Myrt is still, in Darla's words, "a power-house." Darla, a middle school teacher in Luling, has lived in St. Charles Parish her entire life so far, with the exception of her college years spent at, well . . . LSU.

The week before Katrina, I was dealing with my husband (Michael) being asked to go to Florida to work—Katrina was about to hit the lower part of Florida before going into the Gulf . . . He began working at the Emergency Response Center for the state of Florida where he received first-hand information about the hurricane track. He—who *never* evacuates for hurricanes—was telling me that we needed to evacuate.

As soon as I got the call from school on Friday stating that school would be canceled for Monday and Tuesday, I was ready to go. Saturday morning, around 5:00 a.m., I called my mom and told her to get ready to go to my sister Deena's house (she lived in League City, Texas) . . . Like Michael, she never wants to leave her home for hurricanes, but for some reason she knew that she had to go for this one. While the kids slept, I moved all of the patio furniture into the garage along with anything that I thought might get picked up by the wind.

I didn't take any photos or any sentimental things with me. I packed very lightly, loaded up the kids and my twelve-year-old sheltie, picked up my parents in Norco, and headed for Houston, Texas. We had no problem getting to my sister's house in League City—we left at the right time. My other sister, Donna, was coming to meet us with her family, but they got stuck in horrible traffic for hours. She stopped in Lafayette at her husband's niece's house where they would ride out the storm.

As I watched the news, I can remember thinking that I was glad that I left. I didn't like the fact that I couldn't watch our news stations—it wasn't familiar faces giving us the news. I became obsessed with getting information, waking up all hours of the night to see what was happening. It is hard to explain the feelings that I had—I had a feeling of relief because I knew that my house was okay, but also a feeling of panic and concern about all of the water, people on the roofs, crime, etc. It was hard not to cry when watching everything unfolding.

I could not speak with anyone except my husband in Florida. He was the go-between person that could speak with everyone. Texting was the only way to contact anyone (texting wasn't as common as it is now, but I learned really quickly!). I do remember that my principal was the only person that was able to get her call through to me. It was great to hear her voice.

My mother really wanted to go back home as soon as the storm passed, but I thought it was best to wait until the electricity was back on, and I finally convinced her of that. My in-laws returned home right after the storm. They checked out all of our houses and cleaned out the refrigerator and freezers in all of the houses. They were able to save and cook some of the meats that were still frozen from our freezers. They lived for few days with only a generator and gas stove.

We were in the Houston area one week before the electricity was restored to my neighborhood; then we finally headed back home. We stocked up with groceries because we knew that no stores would be open.

As we headed back home we noticed a caravan of army hummers and jeeps – I think we counted over seventy of them! I am not sure where they came from but they were definitely headed to the New Orleans area. As we approached the St. Charles Parish line, traffic came to a stop. We had to show proof that we lived in the parish in order to get in. My sister, Donna, was heading our way to stay with our parents, only to be turned away at the parish line; she was very upset.

When we got home it was dark; I really couldn't see what had happened until the next morning. It was quite devastating. My house had very minor damage, though there was lots of debris in the yard, with large tree branches down. Neighbors rallied together to help each other clean yards of debris. Large dumpsters were put in neighborhoods for all of the trash and refrigerator and freezer garbage. It was hard getting things back in order with Michael being gone, and it really drove him crazy not being able to come home.

Police and military were stationed all over the parish. I remember being really worried about safety. MRE's and ice were available at the parks at the Mississippi River bridge. As you drove through the parish line, soldiers were there to help you. All you did was open your trunk, and they'd load it up.

All of the stores that opened had soldiers stationed by the front doors with guns, letting in only a few customers at a time. It was like something out of a movie; very scary – very surreal. I couldn't believe it was like this, and I remember thinking, "When will things get back to normal?"

My school opened about a week-and-a-half after we returned home. Teachers went back a day before the students. My school was a brand new school, and the military was using it as a make-shift base. The gym was wall-to-wall cots for the soldiers to sleep on. Rooms were labeled "chapel," "infirmary," "general," etc. When the school opened again, many students were absent, and some of those would never come back because they relocated to another area.

Being back to work/school helped us get a little normalcy back in our lives. St. Charles Parish did a great job getting the parish back up and running. We didn't lose jobs, and income kept coming in for us. We were very, very fortunate. When Michael finished his job in Florida, he came home to work on the demolition of the houses in the Ninth Ward – that was such a hard-stricken area; so sad to see all of the devastation. It was sad seeing all of the surrounding areas going through terrible times. Everywhere we drove we saw help wanted signs, vacant houses, and houses with spray paint on them. We didn't know how long it would take for New Orleans to "come back."

Well, here we are in 2010 – hard to believe it has been five years. The city seems to be back … and the Saints won the Super Bowl! I just hope we don't ever have to go through anything like that again.

Rachelle Crain

Rachelle and I were members of the Colonial Regiment together. The Colonial Regiment was the name of the marching band/dance team/color guard at John Curtis Christian School in River Ridge. Rachelle was on the dance team, and she was a great "anti-pop" music comrade. In early 1983, a young Irish band – on its first-ever tour of America – came to play at a club on a riverboat in New Orleans. Rachelle and another friend told me about this young band; they introduced me to the band's music; and, ever since then, I've been a big fan of U2. She was a funny and intelligent friend with great musical tastes. Even today, I can't read about, talk about, or listen to U2 without remembering Rachelle Crain.

Rachelle grew up in Old Metairie and lived in the River Parishes region for twenty-seven years. She has now lived outside of Louisiana for almost twenty years; she resides in Grapevine, Texas, which is where she was living when Katrina came around.

In the week leading up to Katrina, I watched the news constantly. I can't remember exactly what the news was saying, only that we all kept a keen eye on what was happening in the Gulf. All of my family still lived in New Orleans – my parents in Old Metairie (in the same house that I grew up in); one of my sisters lived in Kenner; and my niece in River Ridge (about a couple of blocks from John Curtis School).

I never believed the hurricane would hit my beloved city, because I never thought anything bad could happen to such a wonderful place. Well, my parents – for the first time in their lives – actually evacuated for a hurricane. They evacuated to Tylertown, Mississippi – that's where my dad grew up. He still has relatives that live on the farm and on the land of his parents. So, I was glad that they got out; but my sister and niece decided to stay and ride out the storm. My niece actually stayed at my parents' house in old Metairie, while my sister stayed at her house in Kenner.

I was astonished by all of the people that were leaving the city. I was glad most left, but could understand why some stayed behind. Most of all, I was saddened for the people that wanted to leave but had no means to – they were forced to experience something most of us couldn't even imagine in our worst nightmares.

I didn't house any evacuees, but the thought did cross my mind. I was a single parent at that time, with a small child and a lower-salary income, and I thought it best not to invite strangers into our home. Friends and family that I knew all went to stay with other members of their family. I couldn't get in touch with anyone else to invite them to my house.

I don't think I slept for three days … just constantly watching the news. At the time, I was working for a family that was originally from New Orleans. I went to high school and was on dance team with the owner of the company. So when Katrina hit, we all were watching the news and the online reporting of the storm. For that whole week after Katrina hit, we didn't get a lick of work done. Thank goodness I was working for someone that had a connection with this disaster, because I don't think any other employer would have been so generous and understanding for my lack in my employment duties and responsibilities in the days that followed the storm.

My niece stayed behind in my parents' house, and when Katrina was inland, I would call her and hear over the phone the loud rumbling and wind. It was insanely intense to hear that through the phone. She had to scream into the phone so I could hear her. Even to this day, I cannot imagine the decibels the storm created.

I never lost contact with my family. The only time there was a lull was when phone batteries ran out and they had to find electricity to recharge.

After the storm was over, I could talk to my niece – remember, she was staying in my parents' house. No water was in the house until the levees broke; it was only then that water started coming in. The storm didn't cause the flooding, the weak levees did. Once the levees broke, water started rising, and my niece had to retreat to the second story of the house. My niece's boyfriend's mother worked at the time for the Mayor of Kenner. She sent a rescue boat to pick up my niece and her boyfriend from the house. There was two feet of water inside of the house, but when my niece stepped outside and down the front porch steps, she was up to her neck in water. She said she had never been so scared in her life. They had to walk about six blocks to higher ground for their rescue. Shortly after they left my parents house, many neighbors became squatters in my parents' house on the second floor, along with their pets. I don't know how many days they were there, but they eventually crawled through my parents' window onto the roof and were rescued via boat.

Once my niece and my sister were reunited, they hopped in a car and headed to Tylertown, where my parents were. I don't think they were any better off because Tylertown was hit by the storm, and even though there was no flooding there, the power was out and there was a lack of supplies. They had to bear the southern Mississippi heat of early September with little food and water. I tried my hardest to get them to come to Texas, but my father thought they'd be better off in Mississippi.

My parents were literally some of the first people back in the city when the roads and barricades were opened. They quickly gutted and rebuilt their home, and by the time all of their neighbors were coming back into town, their house was completely renovated. My sister's house in Kenner and my niece's house in River Ridge were not damaged at all by the storm. In fact, my sister's house never lost electricity.

Reportedly, nine bodies were found in my parents' neighborhood. Whether the bodies were of residents in that community, or if they floated down Airline Highway when the levees broke, I can't say.

My mother's brother and his son were on the roof of their house for three days before being rescued. He lived in Chalmette, close to Lower Ninth Ward.

My parents have rental property in the Lower Ninth Ward/Holy Cross District. The house's inside watermark was one inch from the ceiling. The house sits on the Industrial Canal. The levee is right outside the front door. I played on that levee when I was a child, and still to this day I climb it and watch the barges float by. It was my mother's brother's house before he passed away many years ago, and my parents have been renting it out since. The tenants that occupied the house evacuated to Texas and they have not come back. The house has now been completely restored and occupied by new tenants.

Katrina changed a lot for me. All of my family ended up going back and rebuilding; I'm not sure I would have had it any other way. Even though I have now lived in Texas for fifteen years, New Orleans is my HOME. It always will be!

If my family had moved away after the storm, we all would have lost some of our identity. I travel back there several times a year, and I find myself doing the "tourist" things along with some of the old rituals of an authentic

New Orleanian life. I appreciate it more. I definitely don't take it for granted. I encourage people to travel there and spend time breathing it in rather than staying intoxicated the whole time.

Kirk Banquer

Kirk and his mother were active folks at First Baptist, Norco. Mrs. Banquer was chair of the deacons there when I was a kid. Kirk, while a medical school student, taught Sunday School classes for junior high boys. I loved Kirk—he loved music more than I did. I loved hearing him talk about seeing Led Zeppelin in concert or about Elvis Costello's latest album. He taught me a lot in Sunday School—not the least of which was that I could love rock music and still be a Christian.

For the first twenty-six years of his life, Kirk lived either in Norco, Metairie, or New Orleans. He now lives in Hattiesburg, Mississippi, where he was living when Katrina hit.

We knew it was going to be a major storm, but we had been through hurricanes before and—being up in Hattiesburg, Mississippi—felt we were far enough inland that we would have some rain and wind gusts like previous storms, but nothing catastrophic.

I have family in the River Parishes and was relieved to know they were evacuating. Unfortunately, some of them evacuated to Baton Rouge, which had its share of problems as well.

Some friends of ours and their four boys from Mandeville evacuated to our house. My niece, her friend, and multiple pets got stuck trying to evacuate out of Metairie and ended up staying with us, too.

When the storm hit the coast and was still very powerful, I was a little apprehensive since the projected path showed it to be coming our way. The storm actually passed over Hattiesburg around late morning I think, and we were terrified as we had 100 mph winds, multiple trees falling onto the house, and loss of power and water. I remember the kids all hiding under the dining room table and crying—an extremely scary situation.

I think I was able to make contact with family after a few days. But we were without power and water for about a week. Grocery stores and gas stations had very little to sell, and most people were busy trying to cut trees to clear roads. It was an extremely hot and miserable week or so until power and water were restored; then the cleanup and house/roof repairs began, and those took months.

I was saddened to see the flooding and mayhem that occurred in New Orleans. Upon visiting the city a few months later, it seemed almost like a ghost town. My family and friends in the River Parishes and in Mandeville actually fared better than we did as far as damage, etc.

Keith Falgout

I've known Keith since I was ten. His family lived on the street behind mine, a little further down the road. We met pretty soon after I moved to Destrehan, played ball together with other friends (in empty lots here and there), and played organized baseball together for the Hill Heights little league (we were awful! There were some truly talented young athletes on the team, but then there were also goofy, un-athletic kids like me—over the course of two "seasons," I only recall us winning one game).

Keith has never lived outside of Louisiana, and almost all of that has been in Destrehan. He now lives back in his old house (down the road behind my old house) with his father. This is where he was living when Katrina came to visit.

The people on the news kept telling us to plan ahead—make plans to get out. Most neighbors were doing that. My first thought was that I had a seventy-year-old father, and that he was not going to want to leave. So, no, I did not initially plan to leave. Why? Because when you have someone that old with you, their mind is made up, and they are not leaving.

I was at work the Friday night before the storm. I worked for the New Orleans Zephyrs at the time. It was our last home stand for the season. We played the game Friday night and planned a double header for Saturday, starting at 10:00 a.m.—that was so the other team could get out of town Sunday morning. The games on Saturday eventually were canceled; the company told us we could come to the field and stay if we wanted to.

I felt it was a good idea to leave, but Dad wanted to stay. At five o'clock Sunday morning, my dad woke me up and said that we better leave! So we packed up the truck and went to stay with relatives on the North Shore.

My sister went up to Tennessee, and my brother went to Texas. I lost contact with them for about three days.

My dad and I returned home on Tuesday. The drive home was pretty rough; WWL radio was on the air giving people updates. The closer we got to the River Parishes, the more my thoughts turned toward my house. You felt bad for the people in New Orleans, but you prayed your house was okay.

Turning down my street, we realized we were lucky. Our tree in the front yard was split in two, and there were a few shingles missing, but overall our house was in good shape. We had no power, but we did have water, and believe it or not, phone services two days after the storm. We had gas and water, but no lights/electricity.

After settling back into our house, my dad and I drove around the neighborhood looking for people who might need help. We were able to get an ice machine to work, and we were giving ice to people who needed it.

A couple of days later, my boss was able to contact me. He was in North Carolina, where the home office is. He wanted me to go check out Zephyr Field. The Army had taken over the field for a base. At first they (the Army) would not let me on the grounds. It was a big mess . . .

My boss was happy that it was not a total loss; in fact, it could have been a lot worse. I got paid for two months after the storm, then was let go for about three weeks while the workers cleaned up the place; then, I was brought back and went back to work.

Terry Gamble

The first time I met Terry, I remember him telling me, "last name, 'Gamble,' like . . ." and he pretended to roll dice. Terry was a junior at Destrehan High when I started there as a sophomore; he was quite a good lead trumpet in the marching, jazz and concert bands. By the time he was graduating, he was also playing bass guitar in a local heavy-metal band named Rex—he had the big hair, spandex and the works.

Terry moved from Kenner to St. Rose when he was thirteen. He lived in and around the River Parishes and the New Orleans area all of his life, until Katrina hit. After Katrina, he lived in Missouri for two years; he now lives in Alabama.

I worked at a printing company on Jefferson Highway in New Orleans. We watched the news that Friday, and Katrina was supposed to hit Pensacola. We did the usual thing before a storm: put stuff on top of our desks and got equipment off the ground in case we got a lot of rain and it flooded. We thought we'd be back at work on Monday. We never evacuated for a storm, so it didn't even cross my mind. Little did I know I would never go back there.

We didn't leave until Sunday, the day before it hit. My wife was the manager of the Hilton downtown, and her boss wanted to her stay at the hotel for the storm. I didn't want her to be down there. We fought about it; her family begged her not to go. All of the guests were out of the hotel by then so it didn't make sense for her to be there. Her boss chewed her out and she cried, but we decided to leave and go to Florida. We left our cat there (we had the cat for about eighteen years). Figured we'd go to Florida, hang out on the beach with our two girls, and then be back for work on Monday.

We got caught in the traffic, and it took about sixteen hours to get to Jacksonville, Florida. No hotels had rooms until we got to the other side of Florida.

Our house was in Slidell—we didn't have flood insurance because we didn't need it. We saw on the news that a hotel near our house had water on the second floor. We thought then that we lost everything . . . including our cat.

My parents stayed in St. Rose; we were not able to make contact with them. Even the cell phones were out. All the towers were down. We were not allowed to go home for two weeks. We went to my father-in-law's house in Ozark, Missouri, and stayed there. Actually, we stayed at his neighbors' house. My father-in-law had thirty (30!) people at his house staying with him from New Orleans. We finally got in touch with my parents, and they made it okay; except they didn't have any power for a couple of weeks. My mother isn't in great health, and the heat was not good for her. My brother and his family came with us to Missouri, also. He has two young children. If not for our kids, none of us would have left.

In Missouri, we picked up a generator and some food and water to take back to my dad's . . . there weren't any generators anywhere around Louisiana. We also got some large fuel containers.

When we went back to Louisiana, we were really nervous about what we would find; we figured a dead cat for sure. We left the kids at my father in-law's house in Missouri.

There wasn't ANY gas to be found in northern Louisiana, and we were getting very nervous—so many cars were on the side of the road; probably just ran out of gas. And there were huge lines at gas stations. We got lucky and found a gas station in LaPlace with one pump that was working—probably because a lot of police and rescue people were staying in some hotels in LaPlace.

My parents in St. Rose were fine. Their house didn't flood. They even had electricity when we got there. When we went to our house the next day it was strange—like living in a different country. Nothing looked the same; on the way to Slidell there were debris, tree limbs, and cars toppled over everywhere. New Orleans East was unbelievable.

We got to Slidell and the National Guard was there with machine guns checking our IDs. Scary. We had to dodge junk in the streets to get to our house. A cemetery is located a mile or so from our house—there were caskets on side of the street. I suppose they floated away from the cemetery during the storm.

You couldn't even see our house with all the trees down. My truck was still there, and it was fine—no damage at all. Our house didn't flood; our neighbors, though, had four feet (of water) in their house. We just happened to be situated on a little ridge high enough to avoid the water.

We had trees down, a broken window, and a fence down from a tree falling on it. Other than that, the house was fine. Unbelievable. Our cat was still alive too! I guess she just drank toilet water for two weeks . . .

The company I worked for got flooded really bad. The roof over my office flew off and everything in it was destroyed. My boss was living in Houston and decided to stay there. No telling how long it would be that, if ever, the business would reopen.

The Hilton where my wife worked was looted and damaged. Someone broke into her office, spray painted stuff on the walls, and even took a dump in there.

We looked at the situation, and with two small girls, decided it was best for them to stay in Missouri. We both found jobs there. Everyone there was great and very helpful. The neighbor we stayed with in Missouri let us live there for another six months until we got jobs and found a house to buy. We were able to sell our house in Slidell.

Missouri was nice at first, but it wasn't home. My wife got a job offer in Alabama, so we moved there. At least we were only five hours away from home instead of twelve! The girls managed changing schools and homes remarkably well. They miss home, too. They don't understand why they have to go to school on Mardi Gras and why there aren't any parades.

Michelle Cambre Seemann

Michelle lived just a few houses down the street from me in Destrehan. Her older brother introduced me to the album Led Zeppelin II when I was about eleven years old; he told me I would never be the same—and, he was right. Michelle and I went through DHS together—both class of '86. We had most of our classes together. She was always full of life and energy, and just a riot to hang around—and she was the "80s" girl. I can't watch John Hughes movies without first thinking of Michelle; I think they watched her to pick up fashion cues.

Michelle still lives in Destrehan.

We were treating Katrina like any other storm—monitoring the news, but not over-reacting. Most people I knew were planning on leaving. Since our children were born, we have evacuated for "serious storms" on a consistent basis, so we left Saturday evening to beat the crowds; we initially went to Jackson, Mississippi, just to get out of the way.

What were we thinking? "Hopefully it will be nothing." What were we feeling? Tense and overwhelmed. I washed clothes furiously, packed a suitcase full of pictures, brought our important papers.

We made reservations up in Jackson with family friends. We traveled there by van, but when realized on Sunday that the power outages would affect Jackson so badly, we left Jackson and drove to Dallas. Our kids were little (ages 7, 5, and 3), so we wanted to keep them occupied.

At first, the news reports were a relief (we avoided the direct hit), but then when the water began pouring in . . . we were just in shock.

My in-laws—because they stayed at my house with my dogs, and we left a rotary phone for them—we could talk with them; you couldn't get through on cell phones, though. I did not know where my brother and sister-in-law were; they were called up by the Louisiana National Guard. Their place of command began to flood (Jackson Barracks) so they were rescued to the Dome—we could not talk to them, though.

We stayed away from home for a week and a half. We came back too soon—the electricity was still out. But, we were tired of being away. There were fallen trees and some wind damage, but there was no water damage to our house.

Danielle Madere St. Martin

Another member of the DHS Class of '86; we shared lots of classes together. I remember Danielle as kind of quiet, but very smart. Where Michelle may have been the inspiration for Molly Ringwald's '80s fashion, Danielle was quiet, reserved, very smart, high grades . . . and a heavy-metal headbanger. Danielle preferred jeans and Quiet Riot t-shirts.

She's never lived outside of the River Parishes; currently she lives in LaPlace.

The week leading up to Katrina was like any normal week. We had the TV on at work watching the updates on the news, waiting for the newest projected track of the storm. I was not really worried—I actually went to a Southern Living Party (like a Tupperware party) that week.

I never planned to evacuate. I had only evacuated once before in my life and that was because I was living in a mobile home when Hurricane Andrew came; even then I only "evacuated" to my sister-in-law's house across Airline Highway. My family just never evacuated. As a kid, my family put masking tape on some windows, boarded up some windows, bought batteries, bottled water, and vienna sausages, and we hunkered down.

As Katrina got closer, my daughter started to freak out. I didn't want to evacuate, but I did it for her. We woke up one morning and turned on the TV, and Margaret Orr (on WDSU Channel 6) had—in huge letters across the screen—KILLER HURRICANE. That scared me. I didn't have a lot of time to prepare; I packed up my daughter and me, my godmother, and four dogs, and we drove to my mother's house in Springfield in Tangipahoa Parish. We left before the contraflow kicked in, so it didn't take long to get there—maybe an hour.

When you leave your house like that, you kind of tell it "goodbye," and you hope it will still be there after the storm passes. My son and my ex-husband boarded up my windows after I left. I tried to stay calm.

We got to my mom's house, and it felt like a sleepover. They cooked us dinner, we watched a DVD (the movie *Phone Booth*), and then we went to bed. I woke up to no power, but everything outside looked fine. I turned on the radio; at first everything sounded like it was okay. Then they started talking about water rising outside of the radio station, and then as time went on, the reports started to come in—WATER!! WATER!! WATER!! *Everywhere!!*

That night I remember vividly Ray Nagin's plea on WWL—I want to say it was to Garland Robinette. It was the only time something Ray Nagin said actually moved me. His pleas for help for New Orleans were heart-wrenching.

There was no power in Springfield; all we had was the radio. Cell phone service was non-existent except for texting. We had to wait for I-55 to be inspected before we could return home. After almost a week, state police would let you go down I-55 *if* you had ID proving you lived in that direction.

The only thing between my mom's house and LaPlace is trees and the bridge, so there wasn't much to see. There was damage, but not devastation. I had to drive around some downed trees, and I drove over a downed power line (which probably wasn't a good idea), but that was about it.

I was afraid of what I would find when I arrived home, but everything looked okay. When I got home, there were some limbs down and there was no electricity, but that was it. It was *so* HOT! It was steamy outside and inside.

By the grace of God, my family was okay. My neighbor across the street went to Winn Dixie—they were letting five people in at a time with flashlights. The lines to get in were extremely long. He brought me back a loaf of Bunny bread—it felt like he was giving me gold. I was speechless at his generosity.

When the power returned, I turned on the TV, and my jaw dropped to the ground. The Superdome . . . what can one say about that sight? Unbelievable! The water . . . I never thought water could get that high. It seemed unreal. The looters . . . people floating merchandise out of stores . . . I felt like I was watching a movie instead of real events. It was surreal. It was frightening.

We were unable to reach my sister for several days—she lives in Kiln, Mississippi. A tree had fallen on her house. The Walmart where she worked on the Gulf Coast was gone—a whole Walmart was *gone*. Someone brought her MREs; my mom managed to make it to her house with some supplies. Another relative brought her a generator.

I had to return to work right away. Power or no power, I work at a small, independently-owned furniture and appliance store in Norco. Needless to say, business was brisk—especially in the refrigerator department. Most people did not empty their refrigerators and freezers before evacuating; when the power goes out and the food defrosts (especially the frozen meat or seafood), the liquid finds its way into the insulation of the unit making it virtually impossible to remove. The smell is horrific.

Traffic was horrible! To get from Laplace to Norco normally takes about ten minutes, but some days it took a couple of hours to get home.

But I was graced by God to still have a family, a home, a car, a job. I have no right to complain at all over a little inconvenience. All I had to do was think of the people in New Orleans or along the Mississippi Gulf Coast, and any thought of complaining went right out of my head.

Amy Ferguson

Another younger band member at DHS, Amy played flute and hung out within my group of friends fairly often during my senior year. At some point during my high school years, a small group of us got authentic U.S. Navy sailor hats from an older band member who had gone off and, well, joined the Navy. We'd wear them at band practices, pep rallies, and other places to be goofy. For some reason, probably for a better fit, Amy and I traded our sailor hats. To this day, I still have my sailor hat . . . with her nickname marked inside it. I wonder if she still has hers (er . . . mine).

Amy lived in either St. Charles or Jefferson Parishes (either in Destrehan or Metairie) for about eighteen years. With the exception of one year in Georgia, she has never lived anywhere outside of Louisiana. She is now a dentist and lives in Pine Grove, about an hour-and-a-half north of Destrehan, which is where she was living at the time of Hurricane Katrina.

We had just completed building our main house on the property and were dealing with ten-month-old twins. Pine Grove is far enough away that we were not affected by evacuations but had family and friends that were evacuated. My brother left days before the mandatory evacuation in his travel trailer. My closest friend from dental school evacuated to her hometown, and all were safe. A long-parted friend did not evacuate until the last minute and was stuck in a thirteen-hour gridlock. He and his girlfriend had my phone number and called to stay at our place after thirteen hours in a car. I had never met the girlfriend and had not talked to this friend in five years! They came right over!

Living in Pine Grove, we watched from afar and were anxious about the storm, but felt we were far enough away to not have many effects from it.

During the actual storm, my family (my husband, our three-year-old son, our ten-month-old twins, and me) and my dental school friend and his girlfriend were glued to the TV. Both of our friends are life-long residents of the Metairie area, so we watched the news and kept in touch with as many relatives as we could. We also had another dental school friend who evacuated to Winnfield, and we talked with her as much as possible. My in-laws also live on our property, and they had friends who had evacuated come to their house.

The storm itself was a hard one at our house, but we managed just fine. My father-in-law's house stands four-stories high, and we found ourselves in the attic mid-storm reinforcing the roof so as not to lose more of the roof than he did. The winds were so strong that we would lose our balance inside of the house while it blew from side to side! We lost lots of trees on the property and lost our electricity, and we had lots of scared kids, but we fared pretty well through the storm.

It was after the storm was over that we felt the effects of Katrina. We had no electricity in our little rural town and no signs of it any time soon. My husband and father-in-law were distraught about not having a generator and left the day after the storm to pick one up. So there I was with three tiny kids and two friends that I hadn't seen in five years weathering the post-Katrina storm damage. My dad kept in contact by phone, and in two days we had a generator! Yeah!

A couple of days after the storm, with New Orleans underwater, that's when the people showed up—for the next three months we had twenty-three people living with us in our new home. Now, we had some space, but we had just finished construction so not a lick of furniture was in sight. We had mattresses on the floor wherever we could put one.

One of my friends left Winnfield, Louisiana, to come to my house after seeing that her office and her practice were covered in water up to the roof—horrible news for her, since she had purchased it less than one year prior to Katrina. She showed up devastated because she knew that there was no hope of returning to her practice. Within three days my practice was open again, and I went back to work. My two dental school friends could not return to work and therefore had no income. At that point, they both came to my practice. I slowed my schedule and pretty much told my staff and patients that we had two new doctors, and they would be with us until they recovered from Katrina. My friend who had evacuated first worked and lived with us for one-to-two months and still has a bedroom at my house and works one day a week with us. My kids are older now but still know that every Wednesday, Mr. Tim comes to sleep at our house for his workday on Thursday.

My friend from Winnfield was a different story. She lost everything professionally and was seven months pregnant when the storm hit. She lived with us for one-and-a-half years. Over that time period, we helped her and her husband rebuild their lives. Her husband commuted weekly to maintain his job while she lived with us. We helped her through a professional bankruptcy and then get reestablished. We remodeled a dental practice in Baton Rouge, and now she practices in Baton Rouge. They live between Baton Rouge and New Orleans—her husband still works in New Orleans at the same job he had before the storm. She is now doing great but never stepped foot back in her old practice. She always said that she would never go back. She and her husband visit us on a regular basis.

These days, I have the largest generators in our little town. My friends are settled down finally after Katrina. My kids hate rainstorms, and we'll always have our memories. My son and I just went on a field trip and watched the IMAX movie *Hurricane on the Bayou.* It brought back memories of the storm, and not all of them were great. I think my son almost cried. We like the better memories—like how we have better friends and family after the storm.

Bryan Ward

Bryan played trumpet in the bands with me at DHS. He lived in the New Orleans and/or the River Parishes region for twenty-three years. His initial thoughts about Katrina were, "It's another hurricane. Get water, food, batteries, gas up the car, and start boarding up windows."

He was living in Baton Rouge at the time of Hurricane Katrina; presently he lives in Denham Springs, LA.

I honestly don't remember that much from the news. I was more in contact with my mother and father at the time. My parents and I were worried about the point of impact. My mother worked in the medical field and would have to ride out the storm in the hospital where she worked. That's not a pleasant thought—knowing your parents and last remaining grandparent would be in a hospital in the direct path of a hurricane.

Being in Baton Rouge, I wasn't as worried for my own safety. The people I work with told me that flooding wasn't an issue in Baton Rouge; though I could expect power outages and some trees down (that was a big shock coming from St. Rose which gets a few feet of water whenever a thunderstorm hits). I contacted my friends who lived in Thibodaux and told them they were welcome to stay with me if they wanted to evacuate. My friends came and stayed for a couple of days.

We lost power in Baton Rouge pretty quickly. I heard reports of flooding in New Orleans (not out of the ordinary, since the pumps couldn't even handle a thunderstorm) and eventually discovered that a levee had failed and massive flooding had occurred. I was shocked; nothing like that had ever happened in my twenty-three years in New Orleans. I then heard about people on their roofs waiting to be airlifted out. That's pretty scary if you think about it—you are surrounded by water and no place to go. The later reports of people actually shooting at the rescue helicopters disgusted me.

I had limited contact with family and friends—only when the cell phone towers were working and a signal would get through.

My parents and grandmother ended up being taken from the hospital by boat and then airlifted to various locations. My father was sent in one direction, and he eventually just got up and left the holding area and walked home to St. Rose. My mother and elderly grandmother were not allowed to stay together, either. My mother was left on the side of I-10 and Clearview, and my grandmother was airlifted to the Louis Armstrong International Airport. My mother was put on a bus with a co-worker and shuttled to Houston, Texas. I received a call from her a couple of days after Katrina made landfall. The conversation went something like, "On bus to Astrodome. Help. Phone battery low." I don't remember the call verbatim but that was pretty close.

I drove to Houston and found my mom and co-worker, and I brought them back to Baton Rouge. Once back in Baton Rouge, I managed to get a call to my father. He was back in St. Rose, with power and running water, and no damage to the house . . . but he needed food. My mom and I stocked up with a carload of supplies and headed to St. Rose the next day.

On the way to St. Rose, my cell phone rang—it was my boss saying that someone called from a nursing home outside of Lafayette, and that they claimed to have my mother (it was in fact my grandmother). After dropping off supplies for my father, my mother and I headed to Lafayette to rescue my grandmother. My grandmother could only remember that her grandson worked for a printing company in Baton Rouge; a lady who worked at the nursing home took it upon herself to call every printing company in the phone book until she found me.

It took two or three days to actually get my family back together. My friends all stayed in contact via text messaging.

Yes, Katrina changed a few things for me—my preparedness level has increased. I have an evacuation plan, and I am quick to get supplies with the possibility of a hurricane coming to the area. Other than that . . . I actually feel pretty safe in Baton Rouge.

Cesar Romero

Cesar was another fellow band member at DHS, also class of 1986, and in many, many classes with me from our sophomore through senior years. Teachers were able to brag on having two famous old Hollywood screen stars in their classes: Cesar Romero and Robert Montgomery (Mrs. Chaisson insisted on calling me by my formal name). Cesar had a great sense of humor, and he played a mean clarinet.

Cesar is from St. Rose; but he's lived about the last several years outside of Louisiana. He now lives in Tuscon, Arizona, which is where he was living during Hurricane Katrina. However, at the time Katrina hit, he was in New York City—on a business trip.

My family and friends were going to "ride out" the storm. They didn't think anything of it. It was an almost, "here we go again," way of thinking—nothing bad has happened before; nothing bad was going to happen, just a lot of rain and some flooding.

At first I didn't blink an eye, didn't think twice about it; but the closer it got, the more I became worried because it was a direct hit to the city. I was watching WWL-TV online when they pulled (retired meteorologist) Nash Roberts out from the cobwebs, and then I knew the city was in trouble. *(For the record, Nash Roberts was a living legend in New Orleans; he started doing weather forecasts there in 1948. He passed away in 2010.)*

I felt helpless, anxious, and angry. I tried to get my family and friends to head for higher ground, but they felt that it was better if the whole family stayed together at my aunt's house in Metairie. They felt that because her area never flooded and because it was a two-story house, they would be safe. Some family went to Baton Rouge, but my immediate family "rode out" the storm.

I offered my home to anyone; but unfortunately, I was over 1,500 miles away—so it wasn't an easy trip. No one took me up on the offer. But over the following months I did have a lot of visitors who just wanted to get away from there for a while.

While watching everything on TV and online, I felt completely at wits' end. I could not believe what I was seeing or hearing. I felt helpless . . . embarrassed that I couldn't help anyone. And I was angry at how New Orleans was being portrayed in the media.

The day Katrina made landfall, I couldn't contact anyone. All circuits were busy. After that, it was sporadic—they had to call me. Because they lost power, cell phones were the only means of communication, and cell phone batteries were dying. I could not get hold of some family and close friends—for some family members, it was a couple of days. For some friends, it was over a week before we had contact.

Katrina changed the way I look at any natural disaster. It made me more empathetic to other areas that have been hit hard by Mother Nature. It also made me value my close relationships even more.

It also made me despise the Bush administration. I'm a registered independent and have always been supportive of any president, no matter what party, but at that point I wanted Bush out. He was so "smug" on television saying "good job, Brownie," and was so uninformed—and then ultimately shifted the blame on everyone but his administration.

I've always had a love/hate relationship with New Orleans—hate it when I'm there, love it when I'm not. Katrina made me appreciate the city's uniqueness and culture.

Quintin Gerard W.

Quintin was the drum major at Destrehan High when I transferred there for my sophomore year. It was his senior year, and for a senior, he was very calm and very self-disciplined. Even at age eighteen, Quintin could work magic on his saxophone; he emanated a quiet, controlled form of coolness—and it came as no surprise that he is now a professional jazz musician.

For most of his life, he has lived in the River Parishes. He has lived in Los Angeles, New Jersey and Florida, however. Presently, he lives in LaPlace—which is where he was living at the time of Hurricane Katrina.

The week before, no one really was paying attention because they thought the hurricane was going to hit Florida and not us. My thoughts were the same as everyone else: "Just another hurricane," and "it's that time of year again." I never planned to evacuate because, like everyone that grew up here, we are simply used to "riding them out."

I was saying to myself, "maybe I should have left," but I thought about all of the traffic and thought, "I'm glad I'm home and not out on the road." I was feeling very anxious when the storm turned into a Category 5—I had never seen anything like that before! I still never planned to leave, though; I was prepared to stay! And, I stayed home and rode it out. After the storm, all of the neighbors helped each other out!

I didn't see any news or anything for four days after the storm because all of the power was out. I actually got updates from friends in Florida who called me on my cell phone to tell me what actually happened and how bad it was! All of my family and friends made it safely. I maintained contact with everyone. It was *hot*, though!

My house was fine, but we sustained substantial roof and wind damage, as did everyone else. My work status is the same as it was before the storm—I'm self-employed. I know people who are still a few struggling to put back the pieces. My life, though, is back to normal.

Troy Lowry

Troy and I graduated together—DHS, class of 1986. We probably met my first day of school at DHS, when I started there my sophomore year. We had almost every class together, and in those classes where seats were assigned alphabetically, we were always sitting close to each other (sometimes right next to each other—which made for fun in class). Troy and I always talked about Hulk Hogan, Andre the Giant, Captain Lou Albano, and the other stars of the mid-eighties' World Wrestling Federation. And he was as big of a ZZ Top fan as I was.

Troy grew up in Norco and lived in St. Charles Parish for twenty-six years. He lived for five years in Texas, but now makes his home in the town of Prairieville (Ascension Parish). At the time of Hurricane Katrina, Troy and his family (wife, daughter, and a new-born son) were living in League City, Texas.

News out of the Houston area was gloom and doom for the New Orleans region. The first minutes of each news broadcast focused on the oncoming hurricane. Some people on the local radio talk shows kept mentioning that the news media were using scare tactics. My family and friends were scared, and most of them were planning to leave town.

Initially, I thought as I always did growing up in that area—that the hurricane would miss the region, and it would be nothing more than a rain/wind event with some flooding in the low-lying areas. I felt helpless (watching all the reports), but still I did not believe it would be a direct hit.

Soon we were housing my mother-in-law and my wife's friend, friend's son, and friend's mom and dad.

I felt totally helpless, and I must say that for the first time I could recall, I cried openly watching the news. At work that Monday morning all

I could do was glean what I could from the local news, radio, and Internet. I was pretty much addicted to the news 24/7.

My mother-in-law was frantic because of all the reported flooding in her region (Kenner). I was able to find aerial photos posted on WWL-TV's website and show her that her fence was down, the roof had some damage, but that she didn't flood. I'll never forget the pictures of the pools with brown water. Pools closest to her home were still blue, and based on that and the debris line being about one foot from her door, I was able to determine that her house did not flood (and, it didn't). Kudos to WWL-TV for posting those photos!

I was thoroughly disgusted with people calling the local talk radio in Houston. They called to request the radio station play "When the Levee Breaks" by Led Zeppelin. It was also amazing to hear the stories on the Houston news and national reports about why New Orleans should not be rebuilt. San Antonio openly courted and wanted the Saints; Galveston wanted Mardi Gras; Houston wanted Jazz Fest. It made me feel resentful to these regions, and I still hold some of that resentment today. My Louisiana blood boiled over big time, and I never felt prouder to call Louisiana my home as I did then. To kick someone when they are down is one thing but to steal that which is ours . . . NEVER!

Evacuees ("Katricians" as they were "affectionately" called in Houston) were blamed for all sorts of problems in Houston. If a crime was committed in the Houston area by someone who fled New Orleans, the headlines were "Katrina evacuee wanted . . ."

I cannot imagine talking about the Saints and not thinking/talking about Katrina. I vividly recall New Orleans after Katrina, and keeping the Saints was right up there with repairing New Orleans. Sadly, I never was a big Saints fan growing up and was only a casual fan up until Katrina.

Katrina changed that as my New Orleans pride swelled over when they reached the NFC championship game. I became a fan and even bought my first Saints shirt and hat. I have several hats and shirts now (but the numbers pale in comparison to my purple and gold collection!).

The Saints' Super Bowl season put a lot of smiles on the faces of fans in and around the Gulf Coast. It also made me pause to remember lost loved ones who were ardent Saints fans but did not live to see the boys win it all. A dear friend passed away in July 1999, and she was one of the biggest Saints fans I knew. I'm sure she was wearing her black and gold and leading the second line procession in Heaven after the game. I also will never forget my five-year-old son singing (the K. Gates song) "Black and Gold in the Super Bowl" every time he saw Saints' memorabilia in a store.

AJ Caruso

AJ Caruso and I met at John Curtis Christian School—probably when we were in the fifth grade (that's when I started there). We sat close to each other in a lot in classes, doodled in our notebooks about our favorite rock bands when we should've been paying attention in class, and we were always talking about music. After ninth grade, I transferred over to Destrehan High School, but I ran into AJ again—he was in the local band Rex with my Destrehan friend Terry Gamble.

AJ was born in New Orleans and lived for thirty-two straight years either in New Orleans, Metairie, Kenner, or St. Rose. He's lived outside of Louisiana for about ten years; the first two in Charlotte, North Carolina, and the last eight in Atlanta, Georgia.

He was living in Atlanta—working at a hospital-supplies company and making music as a free-lance artist and composer—when Katrina's winds began to blow.

I remained very close to the news for Katrina, since it had become such a large and threatening storm. I was in close contact with family and friends, and I was beginning to survey who was planning to evacuate should the need arise, and who was planning to remain in place. If I recall, it was still unknown if Katrina was going to take the "perfect turn" north towards Louisiana, but it was looking like the odds were increasing, and I believe voluntary evacuations were in order at this time.

Initially I was not that worried, since so many storms had come and gone over the past years. However, this storm was building in such intensity that I was actually beginning to worry about those that were persistent in not evacuating if necessary—this had all the signs of the "big one."

Even as late as Thursday of that week I was remaining optimistic, but I was very nervous by then. A few friends and family had already evacuated, but the majority did not leave until the weekend when it began looking eminent. I distinctly remember leaving work on Friday (days before landfall), talking to coworkers on the way out, suggesting that this was looking very bad and that we may see individuals cutting themselves out of their attics if this one hits New Orleans directly (most individuals not from New Orleans had no idea what I was talking about).

At the most, we had fourteen people staying at our house (including my wife, Angela, and me). We also had a dog, a cat, a bird, and a ferret. Since most of them came from Chalmette, losing everything, they were with us for around 30-45 days in total—some off and on. This provided very interesting times for the family since my wife and I were the only ones working during this period—and maintaining a household of fourteen was not easy. Stress levels were already at their peaks. Emotions were out of control as the family watched the news from afar, and it was not unusual for the environment to range from individuals crying at the devastation and loss to family members fighting over who let the trash pile up in the kitchen. Very tough and emotional times for sure, very chaotic.

Unfortunately, my company was holding its annual national meeting that week, so I had to fly to Arizona on the Sunday morning of the day Katrina made landfall. By now, our house was filling up with evacuees with whom I had to leave my wife alone to handle. It was evident that it was going to make landfall by now, so I was really nervous. My mother and step-father decided to remain home in St. Rose, but I talked with my mom encouraging her to make the trip to snatch my grandmother (her mom), who was remaining at her home in the Ninth Ward. She agreed. It took the entire day Sunday for my mother to retrieve her due to evacuation traffic, but luckily they made it back to St. Rose. The only other direct family that remained back was my other grandmother and grandfather, who were staying at their new house in Mandeville (which would hopefully be safe on the Northshore). In fact, they sold their life-long home in the Lakeview area on the Wednesday *prior to the storm*, moving to their new home in Mandeville less than five days before their Lakeview home was destroyed. I remember our entire family was so upset that they were selling the "family home," and afterwards, we realized it was a miracle.

I went to sleep in my Arizona hotel room on Sunday night having seen the reports that Katrina had made a quick jog to the right—saving New Orleans from a direct hit. I awoke in the hotel on Monday morning seeing numerous broadcasts stating that the levees had broken and that massive flooding was occurring. I immediately began calling my mother (remember, she stayed back) to see if they were all right; I could not get through at all. I proceeded to contact those that evacuated, particularly my sister who had evacuated to Florida, to see if she had heard from our mom, but she hadn't. Recognizing that my parents lived right along the levee in St. Rose, I was TERRIFIED!

I tried and tried for hours. I remained in my hotel room and ignored our company meeting until I finally got through just long enough to learn that they were OK . . . before our connection was lost. At least I knew they were all right.

The following days at our company meeting involved creating a "war-room" to help with proactive logistics planning to support the effort that was ahead. My company is a very large hospital supplies company, and I was a logistics manager at the time. This team immediately put together elaborate plans for servicing the Gulf region, given all the challenges that lie ahead. This was a rewarding effort for me, since I knew I was making a difference early on in the first few days. We later learned that we were one of the only hospital suppliers entering the area for the weeks that followed, which again made me very proud.

As a non-resident during Katrina, it was extremely hard to witness 80 percent of our friends and families losing their entire worldly possessions. We wanted to help everyone monetarily, but there was simply not enough to go around. This was the most helpless feeling I have ever had. I have always donated to charities and relief efforts over the years, but this time it hit home! Helping was the only option. My wife and I spent weeks going home and helping friends and families go through their homes, wading in hip-boots through knee-high mud, trying to help them salvage anything possible. I have always been a high-strung person, and I distinctly recall a moment when some family members were arguing over whether or not they should go look for some small trinket. I calmly walked up to them and asked what room it was last in and proceeded to walk into the hot, ravaged house and went digging for it without hesitation, leaving them rummaging through articles outside. It seemed so insignificant in light of all the other things that were lost, but at that moment, I felt I could at least help ease the pain if I could just locate it . . . I did.

Overall, Katrina gave me an entirely new perspective on life and on our material possessions. My wife and I proceeded to do things for family and friends for the months to follow. We did things such as recreating photo albums, archiving salvaged 8mm films that were rescued to DVD, making copies of lost music, etc. Every little thing was worth the effort, even if it seemed insignificant, just to give them back any part of the thousands of personal effects or memories that were lost in the storm. So, what did Katrina change? It changed a lot, and I will never forget that day.

I have been a New Orleans Saints fan since birth. I distinctly remember years and years of literally tear-shedding hysterics as a youngster, watching the Saints falter every season. Flash forward to 2005. Personally, the year following Katrina was the most significant as it relates to the Saints.

I will never forget watching the homecoming game from our home in Atlanta, when the Saints returned to New Orleans . . . and lo and behold, playing the Atlanta Falcons at that! I clearly remember the tears shed that evening watching the dramatic unveiling of the renovated Superdome. This, at the time, was "our Super Bowl." As we all remember, not only did the Saints win that game, but they went on to the NFC Championship that year. I, as well as thousands of others, just *knew* the Saints were going to make it to the Super Bowl that year. It was too perfect, too symbolic, coming off of the Katrina catastrophe; just like when the New England Patriots went following 9/11, right?

I remember watching the Saints play the Chicago Bears in that soon-to-be-historic game . . . and then the first snowflake fell. I knew in my heart at that moment, that we would not be going to the Super Bowl. That season, and that game in my opinion, was the most symbolic as it relates to the Saints connection with Katrina. While I, as well as all Saints fans, were so proud of the incredible comeback made that year, which truly was a feat of incredible proportions given all the team had to go through, at the end of the day it personally gave me that unlucky feeling of "always coming up an inch short" as it related to the Saints. That, to me, was the year the city needed it most coming off of Katrina, but it again drifted away like dust in the wind. That season, the tie between the Saints, the fans, and Katrina were one in the same. They (the Saints) became a symbol of the city's climb to normalcy, that still provided hope, having at least made it farther than the team ever had, despite the Super Bowl miss. Up to this point, it was hard to talk about the Saints without some correlation to Katrina.

This last season however, was different. I know I am not alone when I speak of what this season and the Super Bowl win meant to myself and any New Orleanian. Personally, I do not correlate this past season with Katrina as much, despite what this means to the region in terms of the rebuilding effort and the come-back of the city overall. The interest it has generated for the city of New Orleans has been fantastic and no doubt will help with the continuing effort of restoring life to normal across the region. While no doubt important to the effort, I feel that the Katrina reference may have been used a little too much this season. I know that the news media and others used this to capitalize on the events, but in my opinion, what the season and Super Bowl win meant to the region and all Saints fans would have been just as dramatic and exciting regardless. The "story" behind the thirty-year journey to the Super Bowl—and more importantly, the win—provided hope for a region that has always felt depressed, even despite Katrina.

I think the Saints winning the Super Bowl made everyone (including myself), feel like "someone" for the first time in the Saints history, and Katrina only added to the equation. To me, the season and Super Bowl win (sorry to repeat, I love the sound of that) symbolizes the end of one era and the beginning of a new one—one from the perspective of the Saints' and the fans' journey to finally achieving the ultimate victory, and one that can hopefully close the door on the Katrina chapter.

While this catastrophe should always be in our minds and hearts, I feel that the Saints' Super Bowl victory provided a "cleansing" of some sort. While there continues to be regions that are still returning to normal, and while the population and economy are still regaining strength and continue to get better, I feel the Super Bowl win symbolizes that the region HAS made it through the catastrophe, HAS made it through unbelievable adversity, HAS overcome astronomical odds, and shows the resilience of a region, a people, and their beloved sports team that is unfounded and of which I am so proud to call home. WHO DAT!

Johnette Arendt Spellman

Johnette and I were members of the John Curtis Colonial Regiment together—she was on the dance team. She had a great little two-door convertible sports car, and one time she drove me around the school—an older red-head driving a little freshman like me around . . . it was quite a thrill (for me, at least!).

Having always lived in the New Orleans area, she and her family were living in the Lakeview area when Katrina came along.

Friday night we went to a high school football game at Tad Gormley Stadium—that's the stadium that you probably saw on the news that was filled with water. The Friday night before the storm we were in that stadium with all our friends and family watching a Brother Martin High School football game. And it was a hot, hot, hot night. Saturday morning is when we started to notice the warnings that the storm may be coming, and that we may be the direct hit. I've never evacuated for a storm, *ever*. Katrina was the first storm I ever even *thought* of evacuating for.

But "leaving" for us meant going downtown to the Hilton for the weekend, because every single storm before Katrina, that's what we did—we went downtown to the Hilton, had a little family reunion, enjoyed the grandparents, and then we'd go back home. That's really all we did.

I guess the turning point for me was about eleven or twelve o'clock that Saturday. I was telling my mother-in-law that I wasn't leaving, that I wasn't going through the hassle. She started to get panicky with me—and she's usually cool as a cucumber—and that was when I thought, "Okay, maybe this is something different." You know, when you start seeing the Mayor, and the President . . . I mean, *then* it starts to reinforce, "Well, maybe this is something that we need to leave for."

So, we started packing, but we're packing like any other typical storm—a few changes of clothes and nothing special. A few days, and then we'd be back home. What was interesting was that *something* told me to take the pictures with us—to take the photo albums with us, to take the pictures that are hanging on the walls. And to take the small antiques—like things that were my mother's. I started putting those things away just in the event this *was* something huge.

And my husband, Kenny, went around the house and videotaped all the contents of the house. We've never done that before. I don't know what force told us to do that, but we are very grateful that we did because a lot of our friends that have small kids—they lost everything. They don't even have the photo albums . . . you can replace all the stuff, but the memories that are in photo albums of your kids and all those special moments in their lives—that's what you can't really replace.

But we didn't go to the Hilton. We ended up going to Baton Rouge. My in-laws said, "Listen, we have something booked in Baton Rouge. It's not too far away, you know. It's not a big deal. Let's just go to Baton Rouge to be safer than sorry." And so, we could have gone to the Hilton, but thank God we didn't.

We got there Saturday night. We were some of the first evacuees to get to the hotel. On Sunday, it was jam-packed with people, people waiting in the lobby; jammed with people and reporters from other places, like the BBC—the BBC interviewed me. It was like, I mean, the *world* knew it was something huge, and it hadn't even hit yet.

Katrina hits . . . and we're sitting in the hotel room. Once the electricity came back up, we started watching the news and started to see what was going on. It looked like everything was fine—you know, it did pass over us, the danger was over, and everything was pretty much okay. Well, a tree at the hotel fell on our car, so we were kind of thinking, "How are we going to get this tree removed from our car?" That was kind of comical.

And then . . . I don't know if it was twenty-four hours later or how long . . . the levees . . .

We're seeing on the news the tragedy that is going on downtown with everyone left behind. Our hearts were breaking because of everything that was going on in front of the Convention Center and at the Superdome. I mean, it was just brutal to watch that. We couldn't understand why the federal government or some local government or *someone* couldn't get in to bring food and water. It was horrible.

We made friends with an FBI agent who happened to be staying in the hotel, and we asked him if he could get in before we could (we were going to try to sneak in ourselves), to check out our house for us: "Here's our address. Let us know if everything is okay." By the time he went down there, the levees had broken—and we lived very close to where the levees had broken. All he could say was, "There's nothing there, guys." You know, your home has six or seven feet of water in it, and there are no signs of the water going down, so . . .

So, one of the first things that we did was try to move into action. Kenny works for Brother Martin—a school which is run by the Brothers of the Sacred Heart, who also run Catholic High in Baton Rouge—and he's contacting the Brothers of the Sacred Heart. Catholic High in Baton Rouge was kind of like "ground central" for Brother Martin. Because Brother Martin is over in Gentilly, they got a lot of water, and they were badly damaged, too . . . so all the highest ranking people of Brother Martin kind of met at Catholic High. So, we all went to Catholic High knowing that some of us didn't have anything to go back home to.

Here we are living in hotels, and we're not sure what we are going to do next. I brought all of the insurance policies with me, so I'm trying to get on the phone with our homeowners insurance, trying to call my auto insurance because my car is in the driveway at home under water. We hoped that our house was somehow an island, until we saw Tad Gormley Stadium with the water—it looked like a soup bowl. Really, until we saw that, we didn't believe the FBI agent. It was something about seeing it on the news that made it real for us: that we *really* have *nothing* to go back home to.

We thought it would be wise to get the kids into some kind of formal school, or preschool, or *something*. Get them out of this crazy situation so that we can handle what we need to handle, and they are in a safe place, and they are taken care of, and they are doing activities. As much as we could, we tried to separate them from all of the chaos that was going on.

It was strange . . . we were driving around Baton Rouge and we see this sign "Baton Rouge Lutheran," (Kenny is Catholic, I am Lutheran). We turn into this school, and we walk in and ask, "I know this is a strange request, but is there any way possible that we could get our kids into your school just for a temporary basis while this is going on? We are trying to figure out what we are doing next; we've just lost everything, but we need a safe place for our kids to go." It was totally unbelievable to us, but they were offering *before* we ever even finished asking—"Absolutely! They can come in tomorrow. And they can stay as long as you need them to stay. Here are some uniforms, here are backpacks, and school supplies, here's everything . . ." And we were just scratching our heads—these people were just *so* generous.

Then we started a little bit of a routine: I dropped Kenny off at Catholic High to work; I dropped the kids off at Baton Rouge Lutheran; then I'd go back to the hotel room and I'd start "working" the insurance, just "working" the insurance. We were trying to make the abnormal as normal as possible. I'd pick up the kids after school, and it's like, "Okay guys, you want to go swimming?" and we'd go swimming . . . they'd have a blast. What's ironic about it is they'll ask us now, "So, when are we going back to Baton Rouge?" It was the most catastrophic time of our lives, and they don't see it as that.

We were there in Baton Rouge at the Quality Inn Suites on Bluebonnet for nine weeks. Then, we moved from there to the French Quarter.

Kenny and his brother snuck into Orleans Parish before they should have. He didn't tell me he was going to do it, *which I am still mad about*—it's like, "you don't think a chick can go back and sneak back in with you?" Anyway, he snuck back in with his brother, probably four or five days after the levees broke. By the time they brought me back in, when I saw what I saw, it was just . . . I walked three steps into the house, assessed everything, and I said, "Okay. I never want to see this place; I am not getting anything out of this place; I'm never coming back here. I never want to see this again." It made that much of an impression on me. Kenny is still very sentimental about driving past the house. Now, the new owners have fixed it up and it's lovely—the neighborhood is coming back. But I am *that much* detached from it.

My brother-in-law owns a building in the French Quarter, and he basically said, "Once they deem the water safe, once the electricity is on and everything is fine, you guys can go live in the French Quarter and just figure it out. Maybe the insurance money will come in, and you can actually do something." So, we came down to the French Quarter, which was an interesting experience because it was completely different from the French Quarter that you or I might know—at that time there were police officers from probably every state in the country down there. There were police officers—between five and ten—on every corner. Everywhere there were FEMA people, Red Cross people, men from some government agency. The National Guard was there in Hummers surrounding Jackson Square with AK-47's.

We acted like everything was normal with the kids. We'd go take a stroll to Jackson Square to play soccer, kick the ball around . . . and, it was, "Hello, Mr. Soldier," and, "Hi, Mr. Military Man." We'd go to the river and watch the ships go by. And we'd go have an adventure out and make it the best that we possibly could.

Then I started working for this new position—at a temporary office in Baton Rouge. I am living in the French Quarter and commuting to Baton Rouge to work. So, Kenny was dropping off and picking up the kids, and I was going to Baton Rouge and coming back and forth. I worked in Baton Rouge for six months. It was just crazy. I would leave at seven in the morning, and I would drive back into the French Quarter around eight at night. It was brutal keeping up with that pace.

I would say that we got in here (*the house in which they now live—in Uptown New Orleans*) probably February '06. By then there were more community opportunities—you know, the first Mardi Gras. That helped us. That first Mardi Gras after the storm had the biggest crowds I've ever seen on St. Charles, and it was all locals. They were all there because they wanted to see that; they wanted that sense of community. It sounds strange to the rest of the world, but that kind of helped us connect with one another—because you were just working; you were going home; you were trying to fix your house, or you were trying to find a new one; you were trying to fit the pieces of your life back together. Events like Mardi Gras really helped a lot.

My parents—my parents retired to Mississippi. So theirs is a whole other story. They're in Gulfport. My dad is ex-military, so I figured that there is no way he is not going to be okay. But when Katrina struck . . . He's in his late seventies, so I'm thinking, "Did they get out?" They *didn't* get out—they were *helicoptered* out. That was tough. We were all with Kenny's family . . . but my dad and my step-mom didn't leave, and that was hard. I wasn't in touch with them for, I guess, probably two weeks. My dad is an ex-POW. Even though he's old, something told me . . . I mean, he'd figure it out. And, I didn't worry *too much* knowing that.

We were there when the Superdome opened back up. We were there! We *had* to be there. The Saints are so much a part of the thread of the community. The songs that U2 and Green Day played . . . We heard that Green Day song "Wake Me Up When September Ends" while we were in Baton Rouge, and so you know, the memories of us driving around in Baton Rouge were just . . . just a terrible part of our lives. And then there we are, sitting in the Superdome, and Green Day opens up with it; and I mean, the tears just start falling. I look around me and *everyone* is crying. You just looked around the Dome at people as far as you can see, and everyone is doing the same thing. It was . . . *community.*

I really believe that those Saints players were playing not only for what they are paid to play for (which is to win and be successful and so forth), but they were playing for the community. They were playing for New Orleans. They were playing for the Gulf Coast. They were playing for people who needed something to believe in.

And, the Super Bowl win . . . there's no way . . . there's just no way (*to separate it from the experience with Hurricane Katrina*). We didn't have tickets to the Super Bowl; we were here; we had a house full of people watching the game. And as soon as—*I mean we couldn't believe what we were watching!*—but as soon as we won, we jumped in the car and drove down Tchoupitoulas. We didn't exactly know what we were going to do, but we knew we wanted to be there. Once we got there, it was like a reverse evacuation—everybody was going the same way. They shut down Poydras. They shut down Canal Street. There was so much traffic coming in from every direction. It was different than any other time going down there to the French Quarter—like for Mardi Gras or something like that. It was locals. It was all locals. There wasn't any fighting; there wasn't any rudeness, or people bumping in to each other. People were hugging. People were high-fiving. It was just this community "high" where everyone was kind and loving . . . It was like nothing else in the world.

Sal Scariano III

In the late 1950s, Mr. Sal Scariano Jr. and my father began working part-time for Mr. Hart Wand, the founder and owner of Wand Rubber Stamp Works, Inc., which at that time was located at 740 Union Street. By the mid-sixties, the business had moved over to 406 Magazine Street, and both Mr. Sal and Dad were full-time employees. In 1975, they bought the business as co-owners; and in 1983 they moved the business to Florida Avenue in Kenner, where it still is today.

Sal III, affectionately known as "Little Sal," began working at Wand in the early 70s, and by the mid-seventies was a permanent part of the office team. Little Sal and Kenny Rauch had been long-time childhood friends, and both were now full-time with the company—Little Sal and my Dad handled the office management; Mr. Sal and Kenny handled the production (type settings, engravings, printings, etc.). Two others, Clinton and Mrs. Marie, rounded out the company as I remember it growing up in the 1970s until we moved away in 1986.

Mr. Sal, Little Sal, Kenny, Clinton, and Mrs. Marie continued operating Wand Rubber Stamp Works up to the time of Katrina. Like so many other businesses immediately afterwards, the future of Wand was unknown.

Sal has lived in and around the New Orleans area his entire life. He and his partner, David, were living in Kenner in August 2005.

I'm one of these people that every time a hurricane gets past the tip of Florida, I watch the news every hour all night. I don't sleep. I watch it all because I know what these things do. Like I told you, I lived here my entire life. They kept telling us, "Oh, it's going to hit by Tallahassee because it's going to curve and do this." Then, it was going to be Pensacola. Then, Mobile. Then, Biloxi. I said, "This isn't good". . . it kept moving west. So, I watched it every day. I didn't hardly even sleep.

I never leave, never evacuate—but I was watching to know what I had to do. Because, at the time, I had three different families to watch out for. I had my dad, who was a recent widower. I have one sister (who has four kids) whom I was watching out for—her husband is a policeman, and when storms come he gets put on twenty-four hour alert, and he leaves like a day-and-a-half before. So I watch out for her. And then there was David and me.

But about 12:30 on Saturday afternoon I decided we *should* leave. I was on the treadmill at the fitness center—the French Riviera (the hurricane tore it all apart). The treadmill had these TVs on top; and, of course everybody in the place was watching the hurricane. It got to the middle of the Gulf, and the eye of the storm was perfect . . . the eye was just beautiful as far as a hurricane goes. And all you could see were the clouds covering the whole Gulf—I mean from Texas over to Florida. I have never seen anything like that in my life . . . I mean *never*. And, that's when I knew that we had to leave.

I started calling everybody, "Get ready—we're leaving at six o'clock tomorrow (Sunday) morning." We ended up leaving at four because everybody was so panicky. On Saturday night, the news media had people literally freaking out.

There was David and me, my sister and her kids, and then my daddy. And I had to board up his house, had to board up the office here, had to board up my house. I mean, I've got to say, it's stressful when a hurricane comes!

At the time of Katrina, my dad was still working at Wand. My mom died the year before—Katrina hit almost a year to the day she died. But Dad was still working. He still drove. He wasn't in good health but he still got around.

We left at four in the morning, and about noon we got to Lafayette—which should be about an hour-and-a-half trip—and then we headed north. Our destination was the Dallas area because one of my mother's sisters lived up there, and four of her five kids all lived up there. So, that's where we were heading.

As crazy as it sounds, even before the hurricane hit, we didn't know how bad it was going to be, but we knew weren't going to be coming back for at least a week. I mean, this thing at that point was a category five, so we knew it was going to tear up a lot of stuff. There were going to be roads that were going to be closed. There was going to be no electricity. So even if you could drive back, what are you going to drive back to? You'll have a house with no electricity—a house in the middle of summer with no air conditioning and no wind, no breeze, no nothing. That is why I said, "We're going up there and going to settle in for a little while."

I stayed in Dallas for a week, and then David and I went down to my friend Tommy's house in Houston, for the second week. The third week, my dad and my sister (with her four kids) came and joined us. My friend Tommy said, "Just come on. Bring your stuff. Come on and move in." And we did.

When David and I came back—when they started letting people back into Jefferson Parish—we went out to check on everybody's houses. Those were the most horrible four days of my entire life. My one sister had like six inches of water in her house, but that six inches is as good as six feet—once it is all wet and mold starts growing, it's *over.* My daddy had about two feet in his house (in Metairie)—mold growing up the wall in every room. His furniture had floated all over the house. Pictures that were on the wall . . . the dampness had just curled them up inside the frames. Now, *our* house didn't flood in Kenner. We were high and dry.

So, David and I spent four days at my daddy's house taking out furniture and everything he owned and putting it out by the curb. You have never seen anything like this in your life. In his whole neighborhood all you could see were people's driveways . . . Everybody in the neighborhood were putting out refrigerators, chests of drawers, mattresses, carpet. I've got pictures of me standing neck-high next to stuff; the only thing open was the driveways because you had to get in and out of the house. If you were in your house, you would have to look over the piles of stuff to see your neighbor's houses across the street, and all you could see were the roofs.

My daddy lived with us for eight or nine months. The hard part was finding people to do all the work—there's not enough contractors in the country to rebuild the whole city at the same time.

There was nothing I could do about Wand—I mean, the building was still here or it wasn't. At that point we were in Texas, and it didn't matter, you know. I mean it was like, if you have no house and you have no city, what good does it do to have a business? To tell you the truth, I thought Wand was gone. I really thought this whole building was gone. Because, if you remember, you'd hear people saying that the New Orleans International Airport was destroyed . . . I told my daddy, I said, "Well you know what, if the airport is destroyed, we're destroyed since we are two blocks away."

Of course, the airport *wasn't* destroyed—there was so much news out there that was just wrong. Some of those national news people didn't know what they were talking about. And, the government . . . Man, if we start talking about government you'd have to write a whole other book. Those people were the most inept. They had no idea what was going on down here. Of course neither did the leadership in New Orleans. That's *another* book! *Nobody* knew—that's the whole point. I mean, for two weeks we heard my daddy's house didn't flood; yet my brother-in-law—Mark, the policeman—couldn't get to my daddy's house *because of all the water!* My daddy's like, "Well, they are telling me my house didn't flood." I said, "Daddy, if Mark can't get there because of the water, who are you going to believe? Mark, or these people on TV who are telling you it didn't flood?"

Coming back into town from Houston . . . we had to come in on Airline Highway—you couldn't come on the interstate. They started letting people in at like three in the morning . . . You had to show them your license and had to prove that you *didn't* live in New Orleans, because they weren't letting people into New Orleans. And, you know, those poor people wanted to see their houses, too. There were a lot of people mad because they came back, but they could only get into Jefferson Parish; they couldn't get into New Orleans. When I say couldn't get in—we're talking *Marines* standing there and cement barricades . . . I mean, you *couldn't.*

Now, this is at the very first when they'd only let you in for a short while, and then you had to leave again. Look, I'm not exaggerating with you—I never cried so much in my life. Have you ever driven down a street at night with no streetlights, and you are in the middle of a city? It's scary. I said to David, in the car, "This ain't good. I don't know where we are going, but this ain't good." And you couldn't drive to your house—they had Williams Boulevard and main streets open, but you couldn't get on side streets because the trees were all down. We had to park four blocks from our house and walk and climb over trees that were lying across the street. We have a lot of woods in our neighborhood. Even though it's right in the middle of the city, everybody's got trees. All the pine trees just snapped in half—boom, boom, boom. Everybody who had oak trees, though, they were still standing! They are just a stronger tree. But the pine trees broke like toothpicks . . .

We got into our house, and the first thing I did was to get on my knees and start crawling around to feel the carpet—to see if it was dry. And everything *was* dry. So I knew we didn't flood . . . We stayed here for four days. We slept by the front door on an air mattress—and, guess what? No electricity. We couldn't plug in the little motor that blows up the air mattress.

So, we had a flat air mattress. We threw a mattress off one of the beds onto the floor and lay there.

You know those candles that you burn to keep the mosquitos off you? We had four of those—one on each corner of the air mattress, and we were on the mattress next to the front door. To use the bathroom, you had to go out in the yard by one of the trees . . . No bath for four days. We went back to Houston and said, "My God. We're never going to live back there again. Nobody is ever going to live back there again."

All we were thinking was that if Jefferson Parish was *this* bad, what was Orleans Parish like? And Orleans is where all the business is—and if there is no business, there is no city. When I went back to Houston I thought we're going to be moving somewhere . . . it just seemed there was nothing left to go back to. I really thought that that was it.

But . . . the hurricane hit in August, right? We (Wand) were closed the whole month of September, and we opened the first day of October. Remember, we also do work for people on the North Shore, people in St. Charles . . . and all those people were back up and running. So there was enough work for me and my daddy to come open up Wand; but we didn't have enough work to hire anybody back. We were only working like four hours a day. The other four hours a day, I was at my dad's house ripping out all the sheetrock and everything. It was six or seven or eight months before we had enough work for Kenny and Ms. Marie to return to work.

Everyone was feeling so low after Katrina. You go home at night, and tears roll down your face, and you wonder how much longer you are going to be able to live here because nobody is back; because you couldn't get into New Orleans until December or January. A lot of your friends weren't back. A lot of your businesses weren't back. A lot of the places you went to weren't back—movie theaters, malls, *nothing*. We were so excited when Walmart reopened! That was a *big deal* to be able to go to the grocery store!

And, everybody kept saying that the Saints were gone. One guy said, "They are going to come back for one year as a token, and then they're going to see that nobody is supporting them, and then they're going to leave." In fact, the reverse happened. You know, the season tickets sold out! My sister was on the season ticket waiting list. She was number twenty-two thousand and something. She is *still* waiting for them to call her! That first season when the Saints came back, when the Superdome reopened—*that* is the "Katrina season" to me. *That's* when people could get away from working on their house and watch the Saints for a few hours and feel good. That year they made it all the way to the NFC Championship against Chicago.

Even though they lost, everybody felt so good because they *came back*, and they were winners, and they made everybody else think we could come back and recover, too. Plus they are good guys—the Saints team has a lot of classy people on it.

But when the Saints *did* get to the Super Bowl . . . I didn't go. I was on a float! The Super Bowl was during Mardi Gras. We had the biggest crowds we ever had for a Mardi Gras parade that wasn't on Mardi Gras Day. There were two parades that day—the Krewe of Carrollton and the Krewe of King Arthur. We were the second one. Carrollton went at eleven, we went at twelve—because the game was starting at five thirty. The parades were scheduled to end about three-thirty so that everybody would have time to get to the game. I was on a Drew Brees float—our captain made a float with Drew Brees' head on the front. We had forty-something people on my float, and we were the very last float in the parade. In other words, when we were done, Mardi Gras was done for the day. Now let me tell you, we had crowds eight and ten people deep all along St. Charles—all along that area in the Business District. There were people *everywhere*. When our float was coming down the street, and people saw that big head of Drew Brees, I swear the echoes off the buildings were *scary*. When we got to Canal Street—there were people in between the side streets like Royal Street, Bourbon Street, Dauphine . . . all these people were going down to the French Quarter to watch the game. The crowds went crazy. My ears rang for like two hours after the parade ended. When they saw our float, everybody was screaming, "Who Dat! Who Dat!" Our whole float was nothing but black and gold. Everybody on our float had all black and gold beads. And this Drew Brees head coming down the street . . . people were going absolutely nuts. It was the wildest thing I have ever seen in a parade. It was just phenomenal! I have *never* experienced anything like that.

Kenny Rauch

I've known Kenny as long as I can remember; he worked with my dad at Wand Rubber Stamp Works. My earliest, most vivid memory of Kenny is from 1973: A little snow flurry now and then is a big deal where we lived; an inch or more covering the grass is a major storm by which we measure time (as in, "back in '73, when it snowed"). So, back in '73, when it snowed, Kenny stopped by our house in Metairie. Kenny began throwing snowballs at my sister and me, and I've loved Kenny ever since. He worked at Wand's until December 2012.

Kenny has lived in the area all his life; he still lives one block from Lake Pontchartrain in New Orleans East—where he has lived for over thirty years.

Everybody had the same idea. If you had to leave, you were going to go away for two or three days—because it was just common knowledge everybody usually leaves for two or three days; you come back home, everything is back to normal, and you get on with your life.

My wife and I didn't initially plan to evacuate, but we had an argument, and I wound up going. We were actually at a friend's house (out at Venetian Isles), and we were eating crabs on their back porch. It was Saturday night, before the storm, and we were just joking around . . . "Y'all the storm is coming; this may be the last time we are eating crabs for a long time."

That night my wife says, "Well, do you want to leave?" "Nah, I don't want to leave." Then we finally decided to leave, and we left Sunday morning at about four o'clock.

We made reservations in Tunica, Mississippi, at one of the casinos. We had a caravan of four cars: We had my in-laws, my sister-in-law, and my wife's aunt and uncle. My two oldest boys stayed home because they were working at the Marriott Hotel on Canal Street.

So, we left Sunday morning. We got there Sunday afternoon about three o'clock in the afternoon . . . and we stayed there. The next morning the storm came and my wife tried to get in touch with my sons, and she couldn't because all of the communication was totally down. She didn't know where they were or what happened to them or anything. By Tuesday they finally got through and said, "Mama, we are leaving now." They said, "There is water everywhere. We have to get out. They told us to leave."

And they told my sons to leave, so they said, "Well, where can we go? How can we get out?" They had to go across the river, and then they have to go all the way to Lafayette before they can start heading north . . . everything was closed up. Ironically, we were in Tunica and they were in Clarksdale, Mississippi, because my son's future wife had relatives there. So they were staying there, and we kind of kept in communication with them. Then, they met us in Tunica.

The following weekend was Labor Day, and we had to leave Tunica. Where were we going to go? We had no place to go! My brother-in-law lives up in Virginia, so he called and said, "Why don't y'all come up here? We've got plenty of room, y'all come up here."

We were hemming and hawing and said, "We might as well go, because we have no place else to go" . . . So we had five cars driving all the way from Tunica, Mississippi. It took us two days to get to Virginia.

We were back home three weeks later after the storm. It took us three weeks . . . I was in touch with none of my family or anything. I've got two brothers who are firemen, and they had to stay; and I'm like, you know, where is my family? I didn't know where my parents were!

On the computer you could see some of the damages and everything, but you still didn't know how your house was or anything. They said the whole city was flooded . . .

We were Googling and everything, and I could see my house on the Google site—I saw part of my roof was missing, but I had green around the house, so I said, "Well, I don't have water." Then I went over to where my in-laws live and it was all blue . . . I said, "they've got water in their house."

Finally after about three weeks, my brother-in-law called (he lived in Mandeville—across the lake). "Look, it is open over here, and y'all can come here." So, we drove back. It took us two days to get back. We stayed in Knoxville one night and the next day we drove all the way to Mandeville.

We still couldn't get across the lake, though—you could get on the North Shore, but you couldn't get on the South Shore. But, at least you had the local news, so you could kind of gauge what was going on. They finally opened up the Causeway . . . you could get into Jefferson Parish, but you couldn't get in the city yet; well, we kind of finagled our way in, and I got to my house in New Orleans East. It was in pretty bad shape, but at least it wasn't flooded. My patio cover was blown off; half my roof was blown off—not the wood part, just the shingles and everything. I was telling my wife right before the storm, "Hey, we need a new roof" . . . this was a bad way of getting one!

It was a horrible sight. I mean you cross over the High Rise and the whole train yard—all the trains were on their sides. I mean it was three weeks later, you know, and nothing was even starting to be cleaned up. You didn't realize how bad it was until you actually started seeing it. You know, you saw pictures on TV, but seeing it in person is a lot, *a lot*, different.

Mandeville wasn't too bad. It had a few little damages here and there but nothing like the city. I mean Jefferson Parish . . . my parent's house was fine. But New Orleans was just totally devastated. There was a six o'clock curfew . . . I had to lie to get in. I had a UPS ID, and finally they said, "If you got a UPS ID you can get in." I said, "Look I've got to go get my uniform." You just told them anything to let you in. Once you got in the city you were okay, but then you had to get out at night because they had people all over the place that weren't supposed to be there. You know—robbing, stealing, looting, whatever was going on, it was still going on.

I got in touch with Sal, finally, after about a month—because we had no cell phone, no cell phone contact. Finally, I got in touch with him, and he was in Dallas at the time, I believe. And, I talked to his dad and everybody. I said, "When are y'all going back?" He says, "I don't know, Kenny, as soon as we can get back we are going to see what we are going to do." We didn't know what was going to happen.

I was driving across the lake one day, and I happened to look on the side of me and a guy that works for UPS was driving across the lake. So, I rolled down my window and I asked him, "Hey, are y'all opening back up?" And he says, "Well, we are opening up in Metairie next week." I said, "I'll be there." 'Cause the New Orleans branch wasn't open yet—New Orleans didn't open until the week after Thanksgiving and this was the first week of October. So I was working in Metairie. I was working twenty hours a day, sleeping four hours. They had so much work, so much backlog . . . people were still sending stuff like nothing happened. So all we would do was just take it and send it back. You know, it was just a big cycle, you know.

The next year after Katrina, when they first opened the Superdome back up, I mean it was a big relief off your shoulders . . . football is back! People had something to look forward to, going to the game every Sunday. You're working on your house, you're trying to put your life back together, but on Sundays you had the football game to watch. It was something to do. I know people are thinking it sounds kind of stupid or corny, but this team is the city and the city is the team and the people are the team. The Saints play for *you*. They don't just play for themselves, and that's the way this organization has *always* been. It's not just since Katrina; it has always been like that. You will hear players say on TV, "This is for the city, it is not just for us" . . . and, it's true. It is really true. You can't really describe it.

I mean it sounds crazy but, you know, the Superdome roof blew off! Then, the Saints were like the rest of us—they were traveling. They had to play in New York. They had to play in Baton Rouge. They had to play somewhere else, you know. It was just like the people that lived here—you had to go here; you had to go there; you had family here; you had family there. You didn't know where everybody was. And then, finally, everybody came back together, and we had a big party!

We still have our problems. I mean every city has its problems. Every parish, every city has a problem. But we'll be alright. We will bounce back. You can bounce back from Katrina; you can bounce back from anything down here. We take it and go.

PART THREE:

Full Circle in the Big Easy

(Final Words)

Going Back to New Orleans

Almost since the idea for this project was conceived, I was determined to let the title of one of my early reflections be the title of the book: *Jungian Jambalaya.* Every time I talked about the project, I referred to it by that title. The Kickstarter funding project and everything related to it referred constantly to "Jungian Jambalaya." A few close advisors (which included my parents) gently suggested I reconsider the title. I wasn't interested.

While finishing this manuscript, my wife (Jency) and I took a few days of much-needed vacation in celebration of our 24th wedding anniversary. One of my old high school friend's parents have a guest house out in St. John the Baptist Parish, and Jency and I went there for rest, to get away from it all, and to walk the streets of my youth. We didn't visit anyone (except briefly with my friend's parents, of course). Instead, we spent our days walking around the French Quarter and driving all around New Orleans. We drove by my old schools and churches. We drove up and down the streets where I used to live in Metairie and Destrehan. We walked along the levee in Destrehan and looked out over the Mississippi River. We searched for the alligator living in the swampy marsh just a few feet away from our hosts' guesthouse. And we, in the words of the legendary Funky Meters, "went on down to the Audubon Zoo . . ." Simply put, we just soaked it all in.

In Part One of this collection, in the very reflection titled "Jungian Jambalaya," I wrote:

> The late Trappist monk Thomas Merton writes about trying to be still to let God do some work in one's self . . . I was disconnected with my past. It was as if I had lived two lives—the first eighteen years in Louisiana (up through high school), and then everything since 1986 when my family moved to Tennessee, and I went off to college, got married, had kids, etc. Maybe God was making whole this divided, schizophrenic self.

I have indeed felt that since Hurricane Katrina, that was exactly what God was doing. Things truly began coming around full circle for me when, in July 2011, I was invited to preach a Sunday morning sermon at St. Charles Avenue Baptist Church.

When Jency and I returned from our anniversary trip, I was refreshed and re-energized, and ready to complete this manuscript. As my parents and I swapped chapters back and forth for reading and editing, the theme that began to emerge was that of the New Orleans region being home. Not just for me, but for everyone who shared their story. Most everyone, whether physically or emotionally (or both), lost their footing and their sense of "home" during and following Katrina, and everyone spoke of returning: Returning to the region, or the return of the region's character to the American landscape.

That's when the old, old song "Goin' Back to New Orleans" (performed with perfection by Dr. John with friends like Pete Fountain, Al Hirt, and the Neville Brothers) started playing over and over again in my head. "Jungian Jambalaya" is of course a part of this overall story, but the over-arching theme of this book—from start to finish—is certainly that of *going back to New Orleans.*

Afterword

I was privileged to serve as Bert's pastor supervisor during his days at Baptist Seminary of Kentucky. I was privileged to walk alongside him as the Katrina stories were conceived. It's been hard labor. Katrina devastated Bert's beloved New Orleans and created emotional havoc for Bert. The desire to write the stories came from deep inside. He had papers to write for seminary and sermons to write for Campbellsburg Baptist Church, but the New Orleans stories were growing in his belly, longing to be birthed.

When Bert first began to fixate on the happenings in New Orleans and the whereabouts and welfare of friends from whom he had long been parted, I feared my student was just looking for an excuse to drop out of seminary, ministry, and life. I had justifiable reasons for fearing such. Up to that point, Bert's history with regard to ministry and seminary had not been enviable. Of course, Bert's earlier departure from a very short tenure at The Southern Baptist Theological Seminary in Louisville was understandable. Bert's eclectic heart and soul would have died in a seminary bound by a too-narrow theology, which holds truth secure within its own box. Still, I wondered. In time, the truth emerged. Bert was genuinely concerned about his friends, friends of his family, and friends of friends who had been directly impacted by hurricane Katrina. The man grieved for them, but there was more to the grief than grief for them. Over time Bert, and I, would learn that his grief was also about his own loss, his disconnectedness—disconnectedness from his past and therefore from himself. My student was in search of home.

Thomas Wolfe may have been right about our not being able to go home again. He probably was. After all, home is more a state of mind than it is a place in time. That having been said, Bert Montgomery reminds us that home encompasses more than a state of mind or a place in time. Home is whence we've come . . . where we are . . . and forever where we long to be.

Bert's trip *back to New Orleans* is more than a trip back to a place . . . more than a longing for a time that was or that might be again. It is a reminder that we are who we are because of the places we've been and the people we've encountered . . . that our story includes the stories of the places we've been and the people we've encountered and the stories of those whose stories help to write the stories of those who precede us. This is a connectedness that we forget to our own peril.

Reaching back over time and reaching deep inside, Bert reconnected with others and, thereby, with himself and with God. Apart from this connectedness, this book would never have been written.

Bert is a gifted writer. In this volume, he showed himself to be an unselfish writer. By inviting others to share their stories, he stilled his own voice that the voices of others might be heard. Bert said it well:

> It's been several years since Hurricane Katrina. Time and space have long since reemerged into the very real present. And thanks be to God, my reality is no longer divided into two seemingly unconnected pieces, but all stirred together into a whole, healthy body of gumbo.

From the content of this book, one would not necessarily know that the author is more than a writer. He is a preacher and, much to his surprise, a pastor. Having been privileged to walk alongside Bert, I saw this in him before he did . . . or, at least before he was willing to admit what he saw.

A word needs to be said about Bert Montgomery the preacher/pastor. That Bert Montgomery is a Baptist preacher and a pastor is in itself a sign of the miraculous. In our day there are increasing numbers of folks who are quite sure God doesn't exist and that, if God does exist, God doesn't have conversations with people. Bert is living proof that God does exist and that God speaks to people. There is no other way to account for Bert Montgomery being in ministry. He has become what he never truly saw himself becoming—a Baptist preacher and a pastor. Thank God he is not a normal Baptist preacher/pastor. He's a new era Will Campbell tempered by Frederick Buechner and carried to the edge by Stephen King. Perhaps God calls guys like Bert to ministry to assure that the church keeps its edginess.

There is an edginess to this book. Oh, the edginess is not in the stories. The edginess is what the stories demand—that we go back to our own New Orleans . . . that we understand our connectedness. It is in owning our connectedness that we find "home."

Rev. Michael Duncan
Pastor, Eminence Baptist Church (Eminence, Kentucky)

Acknowledgments

This book would not have been possible without the willingness of others to relive some terrible and traumatic days, months, even years. Some old friends and acquaintances preferred not to share their stories—they are not ready to talk about it; it still hurts too much. Nevertheless, they offered their support and encouragement, and it has been wonderful reconnecting with them all these many years later. One person said he hoped that reading some of these stories might help him be able to work through his emotions to the point he may one day be able to talk about Hurricane Katrina. I hope so, too.

Debbie Induni not only shared her story, but she donated hours of her time transcribing four recorded interviews—which were sometimes as much rambling and "catching up" as they were specific questions and answers about Katrina. Since she refused payment, perhaps she'll let me buy her pizza the next time I'm down there (hey, Debbie—be on the lookout for Ronny and me knocking on your window after midnight) . . .

My family—Jency, and our sons, Rob and Daniel—held me up during my grief and depression which followed Hurricane Katrina, and they have encouraged me throughout this project. I can't thank them enough.

Finally, this project never would have been possible without the feedback from my parents. They helped me "fill-in-the-blanks" with details not just from my own past, but from theirs, too. From the very beginning, they have answered questions, edited stories, and shared memories. Two weeks before the manuscript was sent to the publisher, Dad was admitted into a hospital in Jackson, Tennessee. Mom and I sat in the hospital room with Dad, and together we "smoothed out" the stories and corrected mistakes, and again relived many memories from my parents' more than thirty years in and around New Orleans. I have plenty more stories to tell, like the time Dad was a Tulane student and was arrested for disorderly conduct on the corner of Bourbon and Toulouse Streets . . . but that's for another book.

Dad died as we were putting the final touches on this book. I can think of no better way I would have wanted to spend my final week with Dad than listening to him share stories. This book opened with a dedication to both of my parents. I close the book, then, . . .

In loving memory of Robert D. "Bob" Montgomery
1936-2013

www.ingramcontent.com/pod-product-compliance
Lightning Source LLC
LaVergne TN
LVHW010105110826
845155LV00028B/488

* 9 7 8 1 9 3 8 5 1 4 3 6 4 *